Doubling
Student
Performance

Doubling
Student
Performance

. . . and finding
the resources
to do it

Allan R. Odden
Sarah J. Archibald

CORWIN PRESS
A SAGE Company

For information:

Corwin Press
A SAGE Company
2455 Teller Road
Thousand Oaks, California 91320
www.corwinpress.com

SAGE India Pvt. Ltd.
B 1/I 1 Mohan Cooperative
    Industrial Area
Mathura Road, New Delhi 110 044
India

SAGE Ltd.
1 Oliver's Yard
55 City Road
London EC1Y 1SP
United Kingdom

SAGE Asia-Pacific Pte. Ltd.
33 Pekin Street #02-01
Far East Square
Singapore 048763

Printed in the United States of America.

Library of Congress Cataloging-in-Publication Data

Odden, Allan.
Doubling student performance: . . . and finding the resources to do it/Allan R. Odden and Sarah J. Archibald.
    p. cm.
Includes bibliographical references and index.
ISBN 978-1-4129-6962-8 (cloth: acid-free paper)
ISBN 978-1-4129-6963-5 (pbk.: acid-free paper)
    1. Academic achievement—United States. 2. School improvement programs—United States. 3. School-based management—United States—Case studies. 4. Education—Economic aspects—United States. 5. Educational change—United States—Case studies. I. Archibald, Sarah. II. Title.

LB1062.6.O33 2009
371.2′07—dc22   2008042303

This book is printed on acid-free paper.

09   10   11   12   13   10   9   8   7   6   5   4   3   2   1

Acquisitions Editor:	Debra Stollenwerk
Associate Editor:	Julie McNall
Editorial Assistant:	Allison Scott
Production Editor:	Cassandra Margaret Seibel
Copy Editor:	Jeannette McCoy
Typesetter:	C&M Digitals (P) Ltd.
Proofreader:	Wendy Jo Dymond
Indexer:	Jean Casalegno
Cover Designer:	Karine Hovsepian

Contents

Preface

THE PURPOSE OF THIS BOOK

The goal of this book is to show how schools and districts can produce large improvements in student academic achievement in some grade levels and in some content areas with the resources already in the education system. By "large improvements" we mean a literal doubling of student performance as measured by state tests. The book provides many examples of schools and districts that have literally doubled performance and references other district and school cases, published in other research, that have accomplished the same goal. In addition, the book identifies the processes and strategies the schools and districts have used to accomplish these extraordinary goals; surprisingly, we and others have found that, though the specifics differ, the general strategies schools and districts have used to produce large, measurable gains in student performance are quite similar, regardless of school size, location, or sociodemographic characteristics. Finally, the book identifies the specific resources needed for the key strategies used and shows how these resources were provided via resource reallocation in many instances. The book ends with a discussion that links the resources needed to double performance with an approach to school finance adequacy that would provide those resources to all schools and districts.

AUDIENCE

The primary audience for this book is principals, teacher leaders, and superintendents, as well as college and university classes that address effective use of resources at the school level. The book also could be used by professional learning communities in districts and schools working to determine how to improve student performance and how best to allocate resources. School board members, legislators, and legislative staff, as well as education policy analysts, also should be interested in this book. In addition, the book can be used as a supplement to a school finance text when teaching the school finance class needed for administrative certification in most states, so another audience is college and university school finance classes.

INTRODUCTION

For the past two decades, the United States has been engaged in ambitious and far-reaching education reforms. The rationales cited for reform include reasons of international economic competitiveness and enhanced civic and family opportunities for individuals, as well as the moral imperative of an equal and adequate public education as a stepping stone to civic progress and economic growth. The goal is to educate the vast majority of all children to rigorous student performance levels. This goal includes high levels of attainment for low-income and minority children, as well as for all girls and boys. The aspiration is to have children learn to "world class" performance standards—to be able to know, think, problem solve, and communicate at high proficiency levels in all major subjects—mathematics, science, reading/English/language arts, history, and geography.

The education system will need to implement enormous changes for the country to attain these lofty goals. Change will be required in school and classroom organization, curriculum programs, instructional practices, professional development, use of computer and information technologies, and the way the system recruits, develops, and manages its most important talent—teachers and principals.

Just as important, the education system will need to use its resources more effectively. To be sure, more resources might be required. But the traditional arguments that what is needed is just more money are not working any more; in state after state where we have worked, the educator arguments that schools are implementing best practices and that more performance will require more money have little if any persuasive power today.

As private sector organizations have had to improve performance—many times dramatically, usually without new resources and most often with fewer resources—more and more policymakers are looking first for the education system to use current resources more effectively. Although many if not most policymakers remain open to the need to provide the education system additional resources, they first want to see the education system use current resources more effectively—in ways that produce more student achievement.

Thus, we would argue that on the finance front, the initial imperative for schools and districts is to show the country, its citizens, taxpayers, and policymakers that schools and districts can use current resources better—that they can produce higher levels of student performance with the money currently in the system. This imperative is particularly salient in the country's highest-spending schools, districts, and states, particularly for those places that have concentrations of low-income, minority, and low-performing students. For example, since the late 1990s, schools in New Jersey's "Abbott" districts have been provided the same level of resources as the average of its highest spending suburbs, which are among the highest spending in the country; today's accountability systems demand that these districts show that their $13,000+ per pupil in just state and local funds can be used to significantly boost student achievement. Washington, D.C., has a similar level of dollar resources and is also under pressure to use those funds in powerful and productive ways.

Again, many districts, including the Abbott districts in New Jersey and even Washington, D.C., might need more resources to educate the vast majority of their students—most of whom come from families in poverty and who are ethnic minorities—to world-class performance standards. Only time will tell. But the first imperative for these and nearly all districts around the country is to use extant resources more effectively, that is in ways that produce a higher level of student academic achievement.

To accomplish this goal, these districts will need to identify and implement new and more powerful educational strategies and better instructional practices, not just do what they have been doing. And if those types of changes were made, the districts could show that they could use resources better and, if still needed, could then make arguments for needing more money with specifics for how they would use those additional resources—for elements of their new vision that they could not fund with extant dollars. This could constitute a new and different, and we argue more credible, plea for more money.

There are several ironies in the traditional and nearly universal call of the education system for more money. First, these calls emanate from districts at all levels of funding. Regardless of the level of spending, it seems districts always think they need more money. Thus, even if districts in the bottom half of spending were provided more money, we predict that they would then behave like the districts in the top half and say they needed even more money. Indeed, this has been the prime response in many states that inject large amounts of new dollars into the school system after a school finance reform. Second, from assessing the research on the education system's use of new resources over time, Odden and Picus (2008) concluded that the education system has used the bulk of new resources for programs outside the core instructional program—not the best strategy if the goal is to dramatically improve student performance in core subjects.

Third, from recent studies of use of funds after an adequacy-oriented school finance reform (Mangan, 2007; Mangan, Odden, & Picus, 2007; Odden, Picus, Aportela, Mangan, & Goetz, 2008), it also seems schools and districts do not use new resources for strategies that we have concluded will have the largest impact on improvements in student learning—such as ongoing professional development with instructional coaches, tutoring for struggling students, and extended learning time. This leads to the conclusion that providing more money might not be the most effective and certainly not the most efficient first step to producing higher levels of student achievement. We argue that this is true also for the calls to "fully fund" the federal No Child Left Behind (NCLB) law.

Further, though our first book on resource reallocation (Odden & Archibald, 2001b), as well as subsequent research (Archibald & Gallagher, 2002; Gallagher, 2002; Odden & Archibald, 2001a) showed that resource reallocation in education is possible, many educators do not understand resource reallocation and do not know that there are ways to improve the efficiency of resource use in education by reallocating the resources currently in the system. Thus, our prediction is that if districts in the top half of spending received more funds, they would retain all or nearly all of their current programs and practices and potentially layer new initiatives on top—a strategy that would not result in dramatic improvements in student learning.

In other words, our conclusion is that the first step for the education system in producing a higher level of student achievement is to create a new and more powerful educational vision and begin to implement it via school restructuring and resource reallocation. Of course, this kind of action assumes that there is knowledge about what works in education and that district and school leaders know what those programs are.

Does such knowledge exist? There is a strident debate occurring within the ranks of those who study school finance and effective resource use, as well as among policymakers and practitioners. On the one side are those, especially economists, who argue that very little is known about what works in education. The recent multiple studies of school finance adequacy in California represent a good example of this perspective. In a synthesis paper summarizing the results of about $3 million worth of studies, Loeb, Bryk, and Hanushek (2007) concluded that, given the lack of knowledge about what works and the dysfunctional system of governing California's schools, the best strategy in the future was to gather more education data and conduct new research rather than provide the system with more money.

On the other side are those who believe we know a substantial amount about what works in education. We take this perspective, believing that there is considerable research on individual programs that work, such as comprehensive preschool for children age three and four, small classes in the early elementary grades, individual and small-group tutoring, curriculum-based professional development, and academic-focused summer school (for a review, see Odden & Picus, 2008, chap. 4). Further, there is increasing research from multiple sources on schools and districts that have dramatically improved student performance, with many districts and schools actually doubling student achievement (e.g., Blankstein, 2004; Chenoweth, 2007; Fielding, Kerr, & Rosier, 2004; Fullan, Hill, & Crevola, 2006; Hightower, Knapp, Marsh, & McLaughlin, 2002; Odden, Picus, Archibald, et al. 2007; Supovitz, 2006). To be sure, the education system probably does not have sufficient knowledge to educate all students to proficiency at world-class standards. But we argue and show in this book that there is sufficient knowledge to start now and make giant strides toward that goal. Our primary evidence derives from districts and schools that have restructured their school program and in many cases literally doubled student performance in the process, which paid for many of the changes through resource reallocation.

This book lays out in detail our perspective on school improvement and resource reallocation. It draws from studies we and others have conducted both on schools and districts that have dramatically improved student performance, which we label in this book as "doubling performance," and on schools and districts that have reallocated resources. We describe the process of doubling student performance, and we discuss in specificity what resources schools usually reallocate toward more powerful educational strategies.

Further, we connect both foci of this book—restructuring to double student performance and the most effective use of educational resources—to some emerging perspectives on school finance adequacy. We also set all courses of action with the process of large-scale organizational change, as both substantial school restructuring and resource reallocation represent large-scale change from an organizational perspective.

THE ORGANIZATION OF THIS BOOK

Chapter 1 describes, in general detail, examples of schools and districts that have, in our vernacular, "doubled" student performance, which we use as examples throughout the book of how to improve student achievement dramatically and use resources effectively.

One question we are often asked is what triggered the movement of these districts and schools to improve student performance so much? How did the process get started? Chapter 2 discusses multiple factors that stimulated several schools and districts to engage in the process of doubling student performance and reallocating resources. This chapter also summarizes the change process that school restructuring and resource reallocation represent.

Chapter 3 delves into more detail about the steps schools and districts go through when they produce dramatic improvements in student learning. We have distilled these processes into a series of ten steps to double student performance.

Chapters 4, 5, and 6 focus on how to reallocate resources for strategies that can lead to doubled performance. Chapter 4 analyzes how several schools and districts reallocated resources to lower class size, usually to 15 students in Grades K–3, though a few K–8 schools also had small class sizes as a goal of resource reallocation. Chapter 5 describes the professional development resources many places provided in their successful school restructuring efforts and the resources required, including more time during the school day for collaborative teacher work on the instructional program and the placement of subject area instructional coaches in schools to help teachers incorporate new instructional practices into their ongoing repertoire of instructional practices. Chapter 6 discusses the strategies schools used to fund multiple extended-instructional-time programs, including tutoring, extended days, and summer school.

Chapter 7 briefly sets the stories of doubling student performance and reallocating resources in the context of the evidence-based approach to school finance adequacy. This chapter shows how the strategies the schools and districts have implemented use resources in ways that are aligned with the recommendations included in the evidence-based approach to funding adequacy, which are detailed in Odden and Picus (2008), Chapter 4. In the context of what schools and districts do to double student performance, what new programs and strategies they put in place to do so, and how that represents new and more powerful ways to use school resources, this chapter ends by illustrating how this would position the education system to better argue for more money if it is needed.

Special Features of the Book

A list of resources includes all the Web sites mentioned in the text, including tools that can be used for resource reallocation analyses. Further, there is a chart at the end of Chapter 1 that summarizes the key features of each case described in that chapter; this chart can be used as a reference when reading subsequent chapters as each refers back to various aspects of the cases profiled in Chapter 1.

Acknowledgments

Corwin Press gratefully acknowledges the contributions of the following reviewers:

Jim Anderson
Principal
Andersen Jr. High School
Chandler, AZ

Marsha D. Baumeister, PhD
University of Delaware
Newark, DE

Melinda M. Mangin
Assistant Professor of Educational Administration
Michigan State University
East Lansing, MI

Melanie Mares
Academic Coach
Lowndes Middle School
Valdosta, GA

Peter A. Sola, PhD
Professor, Educational Administration and Policy
Howard University
Washington, DC

Jennifer Thayer, PhD
Director of Curriculum and Instruction
School District of Monroe
Monroe, WI

About the Authors

**Allan R. Odden** is codirector of Strategic Management of Human Capital (SMHC) in public education, a project of the Consortium for Policy Research in Education (CPRE). SMHC seeks to improve student performance through talented teachers and school leaders and improved instructional practices produced by SMHC, focusing initially on large urban districts. He also is professor of educational leadership and policy analysis at the University of Wisconsin–Madison. He also is codirector of the CPRE, a consortium of the University of Wisconsin–Madison; the University of Pennsylvania; Harvard, Michigan, Northwestern, and Stanford Universities; and Teachers College–Columbia University. He formerly was professor of education policy and administration at the University of Southern California (USC; 1984–1993) and director of Policy Analysis for California Education (PACE), an education policy consortium of USC, Stanford, and the University of California, Berkeley.

He is an international expert on the management of human capital in education, teacher compensation, education finance, school-based financing, resource allocation and use, educational policy, school-based management, and educational policy implementation. He worked with the Education Commission of the States for a decade, having served as assistant executive director, director of policy analysis and research, and director of its educational finance center. He was president of the American Educational Finance Association (AEFA) from 1979 to 1980 and received AEFA's distinguished Service Award in 1998. He served as research director for special state educational finance projects in Connecticut (1974–1975), Missouri (1975–1977), South Dakota (1975–1977), New York (1979–1981), Texas (1988), New Jersey (1991), Missouri (1992–1993), the Joint Interim Task Force on School Finance Adequacy in Arkansas (2003, 2005), the Wyoming Select Committee on Finance (2005), Washington Learns (2006), and Wisconsin (2005–2007). He was appointed Special Court

Master to the Remand Judge in the New Jersey *Abbott v. Burke* school finance court case for 1997 and 1998. He has worked on teacher compensation changes in dozens of states and districts. He currently is directing research projects on school finance adequacy, school finance redesign, resource reallocation in schools, the costs of instructional improvement, teacher compensation and the strategic management of human capital in public education. Odden has written widely, publishing over 200 journal articles, book chapters, and research reports and 32 books and monographs. He has consulted for governors, state legislators, chief state school officers, national and local unions, the National Alliance for Business, the Business Roundtable, New American Schools, the U.S. Congress, the U.S. Secretary of Education, many local school districts, the state departments of education in Victoria and Queensland, Australia, and the Department for Education and Employment in England.

His most recent books include *School Finance: A Policy Perspective* (McGraw-Hill, 2008), with Lawrence O. Picus and *How to Create World Class Teacher Compensation* (Freeload Press, 2007) with Marc Wallace. Other books include *Paying Teachers for What They Know and Do: New and Smarter Compensation Strategies to Improve Schools* (Corwin Press, 1997, 2002) with Carolyn Kelley; *Reallocating Resources: How to Boost Student Achievement Without Spending More* (Corwin Press, 2001) with Sarah Archibald; *School Finance: A Policy Perspective* (McGraw-Hill, 1992, 2000, 2004) coauthored with Lawrence Picus; *School-Based Finance* (Corwin Press, 1999), edited with Margaret Goertz; *Financing Schools for High Performance: Strategies for Improving the Use of Educational Resources* (Jossey-Bass, 1998) with Carolyn Busch; *Educational Leadership for America's Schools* (McGraw-Hill, 1995); *Rethinking School Finance: An Agenda for the 1990s* (Jossey-Bass, 1992); *Education Policy Implementation* (State University of New York Press, 1991); and *School Finance and School Improvement: Linkages for the 1980s* (Ballinger, 1983).

He was a mathematics teacher and curriculum developer in New York City's East Harlem for five years. He received his PhD and MA degrees from Columbia University, a master of divinity from the Union Theological Seminary, and his BS in aerospace engineering from Brown University. He is married and has two children and one grandchild.

Sarah J. Archibald is a school finance researcher at the Wisconsin Center for Education Research. She has a PhD in educational leadership in policy analysis (ELPA) from the School of Education at the University of Wisconsin–Madison and currently holds an appointment as a lecturer in the ELPA department. Her career at the University of Wisconsin (UW) began as an undergraduate in political science; she received her BA in

1993. Next, she received a master's degree in policy analysis from the La Follette Institute of Public Affairs in 1998 and shortly thereafter became a researcher at the Consortium for Policy Research in Education (CPRE) at UW–Madison. During the past 10 years at CPRE, she has studied and assisted in district- and school-level reform, district- and school-level resource reallocation, educational adequacy, professional development, teacher compensation, and, most recently, the strategic management of human capital. She helped develop two frameworks for collecting microlevel data—a school-level expenditure structure and a framework for capturing professional development costs at the district and school levels—both published in the *Journal of Education Finance.* She is the coauthor of the previous edition of this book, *Reallocating Resources: How to Boost Student Achievement Without Asking for More,* and the author or coauthor of numerous articles on these subjects. Her passion is participating in research that informs policy. Among other projects, she is now a researcher with Integrated Resource Information System (IRIS), a project funded by the Institute of Education Sciences (IES). The goal of IRIS is to help Milwaukee Public Schools create a system for tracking resource data down to the school level so that district leaders can answer questions about what works and use district resources strategically to support higher levels of achievement for urban schoolchildren.

Places That Have Doubled Student Performance

This chapter provides background information on the places we have observed making quantum increases in student achievement and using resources effectively and efficiently to fund instructional improvement. As noted in the preface, we use the phrase "double performance" as a shorthand way to describe large improvements in student academic achievement. In many cases, the example districts and schools profiled actually doubled student performance as measured by scores on state tests. Further, most of the examples are of doubling performance from the midrange of performance—from 40 percent of students scoring at or above a proficiency level—to a much higher level—80 percent or more of students scoring at or above a proficiency level. So the change represents significant and large improvements. In some cases, the doubling of performance is for a subgroup, such as when Madison (Wisconsin) doubled the performance of minority students. In other cases, the large improvement in student performance is in terms of the percentage of students achieving at the advanced level, such as when Monroe (Wisconsin) doubled the percentage of students achieving at the advanced level in math.

We also use the phrase "double performance" for schools that increase performance from a point just above average, such as 55 percent to 60 percent of students at or above proficiency, to a position at the top level, such as 90 or 95 percent, which was the case for many schools in Kennewick

(Washington), one of the districts profiled in this book. Such change, while not literally double, represents significant and quantum improvements, especially since improving from a beginning point above the average to the top levels is somewhat harder than starting below the average and ending above the average.

Although our academic friends and colleagues have advised us to not use the phrase "double performance," as it seems too specific and perhaps dogmatic to them, and to use a phrase such as significant or quantum improvements, we have found that the phrase "double performance" is a strong communication tool—it signifies a lot of change. Few in the public or policy arenas quibble with the phrase. Thus, we continue to use it.[1]

Below, we profile districts and schools that have doubled performance. We start with rural districts and schools as most schools in the United States are located in small districts. We then provide information on our cases from medium-sized cities, many with considerable diversity in student demographics. We finally provide examples of schools in large urban districts characterized by high poverty and high minority concentrations. In this chapter, we provide background information and the general story of how each school doubled performance; the remainder of the book describes in more detail the processes used and the commonalities of both reallocating and allocating resources to accomplish the significant gains in performance. Tables 1.4 and 1.5, at the end of the chapter, summarize the gains made in each of the profiled districts and schools, respectively; this table can be used as a reference while reading other chapters as well.

The cases we provide derive from our work across the country on school finance adequacy, hence the larger numbers of schools and districts in Wisconsin and Washington. We constantly were asked what type of performance increase could be produced by the resources we recommended for adequate funding (see, e.g., Odden & Picus, 2008; Odden, Picus, Archibald, et al. 2007). We responded by saying the resources were sufficient for schools and districts to double performance. We then were asked to find and describe examples, which we did; many of which are featured in this book.

As we conducted our research, we also read research by others who identified districts and schools that were producing large improvements in student achievement and also reducing the achievement gap. We reference those studies and citations in the comments below. Finally, in July 2007, we worked with the Educational Leadership and Policy Analysis Department in the School of Education at the University of Wisconsin–Madison to run a weeklong conference on "doubling performance." PowerPoints of the two districts, two high schools, three middle schools, and three elementary schools can be downloaded at http://www.education.wisc.edu/elpa/conferences/WILA/.

1. RURAL DISTRICTS AND SCHOOLS THAT HAVE DOUBLED PERFORMANCE

This section includes background information on the instructional improvement efforts in Rosalia, a very small rural district in Washington; Abbotsford, a small rural district in northern Wisconsin; and Monroe, a rural district in Wisconsin that doubled performance at the advanced level of achievement.

Rosalia, Washington[2]

Rosalia School District, a small rural school district with one K–12 school, serves approximately 240 students. The eastern Washington school resides in a small town of less than 1,000 people with a largely agricultural economic base. The highly mobile (30 percent) student population consists of mostly (92 percent) white students, approximately half of whom receive free or reduced-price lunch. In the past five years, the students and school staff have undertaken a successful campaign to improve teaching and learning.

The performance gains the district produced are impressive. From 2001–2005, reading scores on the Washington Assessment of Student Learning (WASL) increased from 68 percent to 100 percent of fourth-grade students meeting the standard, and from 32 percent to 94 percent of seventh-grade students meeting the standard. From 2003–2005, tenth-grade students' reading scores on the WASL increased from 63 percent to 100 percent meeting the standards. Writing scores on the WASL also increased from 2001–2005 with fourth-grade scores starting at 39 percent of students meeting the standard and increasing to 70 percent, seventh-grade scores rising from 55 percent to 67 percent, and tenth-grade scores growing from 58 percent to 79 percent of students meeting the standard. Similarly, over the same five-year period, math scores on the WASL increased from 43 percent to 85 percent in fourth grade, 36 percent to 67 percent in seventh grade, and 58 percent to 74 percent meeting the standard in tenth grade.

Focus on Improving Teaching and Learning

Rosalia school staff committed themselves, in their words, to implement best-practice and research-based strategies. They started by analyzing WASL scores, established a baseline performance level, and used that as a reference point from which to make great progress. For the first few years, they focused on broad areas and then moved to analyzing the data by strands (student, class, etc.). From the test score data, they set high performance goals for math, reading, and writing; they wanted *all* their students to read and write well and to be able to think analytically. With the help of in-house experts, collaboration time was focused on analyzing the state test scores and setting these high goals.

They also selected new curriculum programs that better matched the state content standards, called the Essential Academic Learning Requirements (EALRs), and the corresponding Grade Level Expectations (GLEs). Teachers started talking about the content they were and were not teaching and engaged in a curriculum mapping process. They wanted to make sure they were teaching the curriculum content that was included in the state standards and assessed on the state test; this would constitute what they called "teaching with purpose." In this process of mapping, they also pulled resources from other districts.

For the first three to four years, the content focus of the improvement effort was reading at the elementary school and then reading in the middle school. After accepting the concept that every teacher is a reading teacher, they incorporated writing into the language arts focus and began to consider every teacher a writing teacher as well. During the most recent years, there has been a strong focus on math with an emphasis on teacher inservice and training. Most students (approximately 90 percent) take algebra by the end of eighth grade, and about 30 percent of students take calculus in twelfth grade. Now, the district is concentrating on improving science instruction.

Rosalia staff also realized that they could make even more progress if they intervened earlier in their students' lives. They had had a preschool program for 15 years but in the last five years had switched the content of that program to a rigorous kindergarten readiness program. They also targeted the program to children from families with low incomes. It took a couple of years to see results, and now, almost all of the delayed kids have caught up to grade level, and the average kids are up to one to one and a half years ahead when they enter kindergarten. By the end of kindergarten, approximately 95 percent of students can read.

Two big components of Rosalia's success story, the staff's investment in professional development and their approach to struggling students, are described in subsequent chapters on those topics: Chapters 5 and 6, respectively.

Cultural Change Supported by Instructional Leadership

Over this period, cultural change drove Rosalia staff and students from a norm of mediocrity to an expectation of excellence. Staff developed a shared mission and vision for themselves and their students that culminated in a living document in which they pledged to *partner* with parents, *provide* a safe learning environment, *educate* all students, and *empower* them to make correct choices.

As described in the next chapter on the change process, leaders in Rosalia have worked hard to create a culture of instructional improvement at the school. For example, a cultural expectation to increase instructional time permeates the school, and when some teachers consistently finished teaching 10 minutes early, others helped them get better at using every minute of instructional time. Another district might allow some teachers to remain less effective at using instructional time, but at this school, the community collaborates and works toward making everyone stronger.

As a result, teachers have taken more responsibility for student learning. Teachers tell struggling students they have to come in for extra help, which is a cultural shift. Secondary teachers are now consciously teaching students instead of just content, and those adolescents have responded to this caring. Teachers greet every student coming into classrooms, wanting every student to be touched everyday. Students were surprised at first but noticed when a teacher missed connecting with them. The fights, weapons, and drugs that were previously a problem in the school have ceased, and now, students are excelling not only in academics but also in extracurricular activities such as band and Future Farmers of America in which they have won competitions. Rosalia staff created a more academic feel for the students. For example, they mirror a college schedule in the secondary grades with only two semester finals per day and let the students come to classes late.

Summary

Rosalia School District has beaten the odds over the past several years and produced large and impressive gains in student achievement by (1) setting high goals for performance on the state tests, (2) restructuring their school and reallocating resources to fund their new educational strategy, (3) redesigning professional development for staff by providing almost unlimited resources for training and collaboration, and (4) reinforcing achievement for struggling students by identifying struggling students early, reducing reading class sizes in the elementary grades, providing extended-day learning opportunities, and implementing a three-tier intervention model. By implementing these core strategies, Rosalia staff and students successfully changed their culture to embrace and support excellence in teaching and learning. Although this district has made significant, quantum progress, it needs to make even more progress and to show similar improvements in all the core subject areas at the elementary, middle, and high school levels.

Abbotsford, Wisconsin[3]

Abbotsford is a rural, primarily working-class town in central Wisconsin. The main industry in the area is the meatpacking plant, Abby Meats. Since 1991, Abby Meats—like many meatpacking plants in the upper Midwest—has attracted a steadily increasing number of Mexican immigrants to work in its two local factories. This external economic condition has had an impact on the demographics in the school district. Enrolling about 625 students in kindergarten through Grade 12, the district has grown from zero percent to 13 percent Latino in just 15 years. The lower grades of the elementary school indicate an even more rapidly increasing trend of English Language Learner (ELL) students. In 2005, the entering kindergarten was 33 percent Latino, a record for the school that had no ELL or students of color until 1991. Despite this steady increase in Latino students, the school has continued to serve a fairly stable population of low–socioeconomic status (SES) students. The percentage of students eligible for free or reduced-price lunch has been larger than half the school population for several years and in 2006 totaled 62 percent of all students.

The growing population of ELL students and high percentage of low SES students presented challenges to the school system, which underwent significant changes to meet the needs of its students and the requirements of No Child Left Behind. An analysis of test score data indicated that the district's efforts were successful and had produced a considerable increase in the percentage of students scoring proficient and advanced over the last four years. District scores in reading increased from 78.8 percent to 93.5 percent of students scoring at or above proficient and advanced levels. The percentage of students scoring proficient and advanced in language arts rose from 73 percent to 93.5 percent. In mathematics, the district scores rose from 55 percent to 87.1 percent scoring at proficient and advanced.

Although overall scores have improved, the school has had even greater success with low-income students. The percentage of proficient and advanced students from low-SES backgrounds increased from 31 percent to 82 percent in mathematics and increased in both reading and language arts from 69 percent to 89.5 percent These scores show a significant growth in achievement in both reading and math for those students most at risk and demonstrate the possibility of serving all students well.

This success is largely due to reform efforts at the elementary school, where leaders have sought ways to respond to the changing needs of their students. In so doing, the school focused on improving instruction for all students and supporting struggling students while maintaining inclusive practices. Throughout the process, school leaders relied on the external support of Cooperative Educational Service Agency (CESA) 10, a regional education unit that proved instrumental in funding reform strategies. The district also tapped the internal expertise of the teachers who were given opportunities to shape the reform process throughout and, in so doing, built a strong sense of professional community. The next two sections describe changes made related to literacy and then mathematics.

Literacy Reform

One of the first steps in the change process was reviewing the district's reading and literacy curriculum. The district was searching for a way to meet the goal of supporting all of its ELL and low-income students more successfully. To reach its higher goals, the district realized that it would need a stronger curriculum that was better equipped to meet students at their individual levels. The administration decided that the basal readers in use were not adequate for this goal and that a stronger curriculum program was needed. The district also knew that developing good reading skills was a key to student achievement in all other subject areas, including a new mathematics program that would focus more on problem solving and application.

When the leadership decided that a shift was necessary in literacy instruction, the state's regional service agency, CESA 10, helped the district apply for a state reading grant called READS to support the switch to a guided reading program. The new program required a substantial investment in professional development, engaged teachers in data-based decision making using formative assessment, and focused teachers on providing more individualized instruction to students. The curriculum also provided a variety of extra-help strategies for students who were struggling.

The implementation strategy was designed to build new instructional expertise and support for the new literacy curriculum on a year-by-year basis. Rather than change the entire school at once, the principal first purchased materials for the first-grade teachers and focused the READS grant resources on those three teachers, who received training and coaching services. By the second year, they had become advocates for the program, and the upper grades were eager for their turn. After five years, the program has now been incorporated into all elementary grades in the school.

One additional benefit, and an emphasis of the new curriculum, was its inclusion of formative assessments to help teachers guide their instructional practice. One objective of the professional development the district had provided over the past years was to help teachers learn how to use formative assessment data in tailoring their instruction to the precise needs of the students in their classrooms. With the help of the coach, teachers have learned how to collect running records of what students do and do not know in the literacy curriculum, how to create instructional strategies based on that data, and how to check constantly to see how their instruction impacted each individual student. An understanding of such micro data allowed instruction to be targeted to the exact learning needs of students and also facilitated conversations with parents and helped the principal hold teachers accountable. The generation of data by the new curriculum not only helped guide instruction but also provided the foundation for in-depth analysis of other forms of student achievement data, including the state test scores. Finally, the principal said that these uses of data transformed the kinds of conversations that teachers have about their work, with each other, and about their students.

Mathematics Reform

Simultaneously, the administration recognized a need for change in the way mathematics was taught at the school and decided it was time to throw out the old curriculum. Rather than simply adopting a new curriculum, the leadership pulled together an internal committee of the strongest math teachers in the elementary school, providing teachers a leadership role in determining the new curriculum. By giving teachers a voice in the reform process, the administration facilitated a more successful implementation.

The committee decided to use a curriculum focused on building conceptual understanding and problem-solving skills. The increased success in literacy bolstered this choice for a mathematics curriculum, which was much more word based than the previous curriculum. By choosing a more hands-on approach that incorporated the use of manipulatives, teachers were encouraged to focus on building the mathematical understanding of all students, as well as providing more individualized instruction to everyone.

Professional Development

Adopting a new curriculum program was only Step 1. The district required concentrated, long-term professional development to enable all teachers to learn the instructional strategies to put the new program into place in their daily classroom practice. With grant funding secured through the assistance of its CESA, Abbotsford expanded the number of days for teacher professional development, hired trainers to provide professional development, and put literacy coaches into their schools to help teachers incorporate all the new practices into their ongoing instructional work.

An integral part of the literacy program was learning how to collect the "running records" or "formative assessments" of students in reading and to turn this knowledge into more focused and efficient instruction tailored to the exact needs of the students in each teacher's classroom. Training in data-based decision making also included aligning efforts with standards and state accountability measures.

Strategies for Supporting Struggling Students

The culture of the school is one in which all students are held to the same high expectations. Those who are struggling to keep achievement up to standards are targeted for extra support. (More detail on Abbotsford's strategies for supporting struggling students can be found in Chapter 6.) Small class sizes, plenty of opportunities for extra help, and teachers who are willing to volunteer their lunchtime to help students demonstrate this emphasis on achievement for everyone.

Other cultural components of the daily life of the school provide additional individual support. For example, the school provides each student with a homework assignment notebook that both teachers and parents must sign each day. If a student does not complete the homework, he or she stays in during recess for a study hall, during which time a teacher makes sure the student completes the missing work. These extra supports may seem insignificant, but the message they send to both the students and the school community is strong. Every student is responsible for completing all the work successfully, and if it is not done, a teacher makes sure it gets done. The expectations are held high for everyone, and the school is committed to providing the resources so that everyone can meet them.

Summary

Abbotsford Elementary successfully responded to the shifting needs of its student population by focusing on instructional improvement, supports for its struggling students, and the building of a culture of shared leadership and inclusion. Abbotsford viewed the changing demographic of its student body as an opportunity to set high achievement goals for all its students, including the increasing percentage of students from lower income and non-English-speaking backgrounds. Abbotsford concluded that to make sufficient progress in reading and mathematics, it needed to adopt a new approach to literacy instruction and math instruction and did so—with the help of its local regional service agency, CESA 10. As the case indicates, adopting a new curriculum was just the first step. It was followed by extensive professional development.

Furthermore, Abbotsford was also able to provide a multitude of "extra-help" strategies to students who struggled a bit more to achieve to standards. It was able to provide teacher tutoring before and after school, more intense tutoring to ELL students during the regular school day, and even three weeks of summer help to some students. These strategies reflected an understanding of two important ideas: some students need extra help even with high-quality instruction in the core classroom and that time needs to be expanded through extra-help programs if all students are held to a high performance standard.

Last, the district built a more collaborative culture of distributed leadership. Moving to a more inclusive leadership style that respected teacher expertise and provided teachers with a voice in decision making helped build a school culture in which everyone, teachers and administrators alike, takes responsibility for improving instruction for all students.

Doubling Student Performance at the Advanced Level: Monroe, Wisconsin[4]

Monroe is a small town, home to approximately 10,000 residents, located in southern, rural Wisconsin about 45 miles from Madison. In 2000, the median household income was $36,922, and the median housing value was $90,100. For the 2005–2006 school year, Monroe School District had approximately 2,500 students in seven schools: one high school, one middle school, three elementary schools, and two charter schools, one of which is a virtual charter school. In the 2005–2006 school year, 95 percent of students in the district were white, while the remaining students came from a variety of other ethnic backgrounds, including Hispanic, African American, Asian, and American Indian. Although it is still a small percentage, the minority population has grown over the past 10 years—in 1996–1997, 98 percent were white. Twenty-three percent of students participated in the free or reduced-price lunch program, 16 percent were eligible for special education services, and 1 percent were ELL.

Two elementary schools from the district are profiled in this chapter, Northside and Parkside; the demographics of both schools are shown in Table 1.1. To boost math achievement at these schools, the district put in place a number of interventions, including an analysis of test score data, extensive research culminating in the selection and implementation of a new curriculum, and school-based instructional coaches.

Improving Test Scores in the District

In the 2000–2001 school year, 68 percent of Monroe's fourth-grade students scored at the proficient or advanced level on the math portion of

Table 1.1   Student Demographics at Northside and Parkside Elementary Schools

	District	*Northside*	*Parkside*
Enrollment	2501	418	355
Grade span	K–12	K–5	K–5
Percentage of free lunch	23	19	36
Percentage of special education	16	16	24
Percentage of ELL	1	0	2

the Wisconsin Knowledge and Concepts Examinations (WKCE), compared to 65 percent statewide. To improve these scores, the district implemented a new curriculum, *Everyday Math* (available from McGraw-Hill), in the 2002–2003 school year and placed a full-time mathematics instructional coach in each of the elementary schools to help teachers use the new curriculum effectively. As a result these and other changes, student WKCE scores for fourth graders in Monroe rose 12 percentage points from 75 percent at proficient or advanced in 2002–2003 to 87 percent in 2005–2006.

Figure 1.1 shows the overall improvement in test scores at Parkside and Northside elementary schools, where the percentage proficient and advanced are added together. As Figure 1.1 shows, Northside went from 74 percent in 2002 to 93 percent in 2006, a rise of 19 percentage points, and the scores at Parkside rose by 24 percentage points from 74 percent to 98 percent. However, combining the scores at proficient and advanced levels masks the most impressive improvements. Indeed, the growth in elementary school mathematics achievement in terms of the percentage scoring at the advanced level is even more dramatic.

Figure 1.2 shows that the percentage scoring at the advanced level at Northside rose from 29 percent in 2002 to 66 percent in 2005, and the percentage of advanced at Parkside soared from 25 percent to 61 percent—both more than doubled! The results show that a sustained focus on improving student performance in the thinking and problem-solving domains can produce dramatic improvements in student performance at the advanced levels.

Monroe School District Improvement Process

In the summer of 2001, the Monroe School District hired a new curriculum director. The curriculum director position was part of the administrative team that also included the superintendent and the building

Figure 1.1   Overall Math Improvements by School

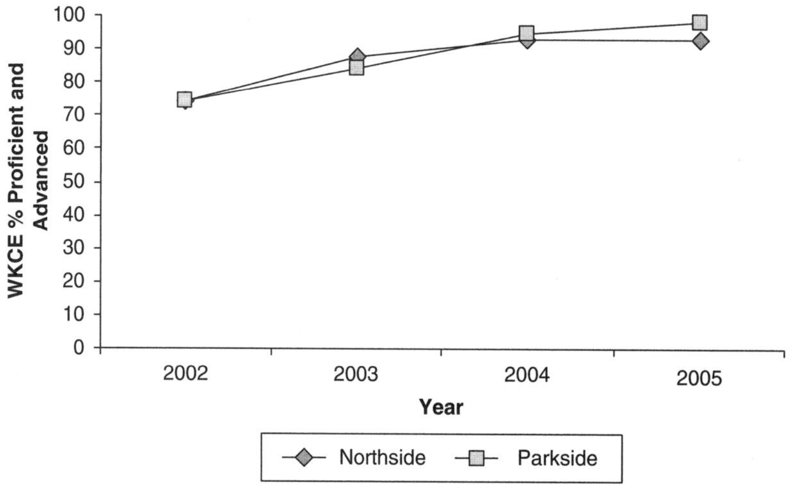

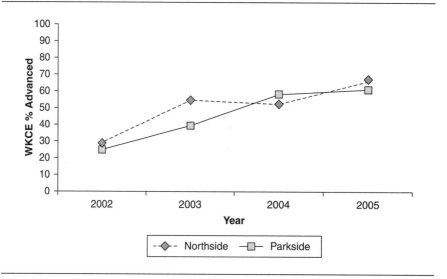

NOTE: WKCE = Wisconsin Knowledge and Concepts Examinations.

Figure 1.2   Improvements in Percentage Advanced

NOTE: WKCE = Wisconsin Knowledge and Concepts Examinations.

principals. The new curriculum director led the administrative team in a review of the district's test scores. In terms of the percentage proficient and advanced, the district's math scores were lowest, so the district made the decision to focus on improving its math instruction as the strategy for improving their students' mathematical achievement and test scores.

Coincidentally, the district had recently put in place a rotating, seven-year replacement cycle for instructional materials, and it was time to purchase new mathematics materials.

The curriculum director then formed a math curriculum committee and charged it with examining math test scores in more detail and researching and selecting a new math curriculum. This committee was composed of 10 teachers, carefully selected to ensure that all categories of teachers had a "voice" on the committee—new teachers, veteran teachers, teachers from each school, special education teachers, Title I teachers—as well as building principals and the curriculum director, who served as the committee chair. The following paragraphs, separated into themes, describe the improvement process.

Educational Leadership

Although the superintendent had been with the Monroe School District for many years, the district made what proved to be an important change in educational leadership by hiring a new curriculum director in the summer of 2001. This person had extensive experience with data analysis, which the district had not used in a strategic way until that point. Her leadership in this area on the administrative team as well as on the math curriculum committee was instrumental in focusing the effort on research-based practices *and* the specific instructional needs of the district. The carefully selected math curriculum committee was also a result of her knowledge of the change process, of how to get teachers to feel that their voices were being heard, and of how to get teachers to embrace the new curriculum and feel energized about the work involved in teaching in more powerful ways.

After the implementation of the new program, the principals in the two successful schools also proved vital to the improvement process. They made such essential changes such as shifting the focus at staff meetings to math discussions led by the instructional coaches. The school leaders also conducted all formal evaluations during math classes for the first year of the program, which was essential to their success with *Everyday Math*.

Setting New Goals

When the new math program was adopted, the district set a goal of 90 percent of the students scoring at proficient or advanced. The district believed 90 percent was a high but attainable goal. What they found in the process of implementation was that an even more ambitious goal was attainable—doubling the percentage of students achieving at the advanced levels.

Choosing a New Curriculum

After disaggregating the math data and performing an item-level analysis of the district's strengths and weaknesses in teaching mathematics, the math curriculum committee determined that the district's math teachers were succeeding at teaching number computations but were not as successful at teaching students how to reason algebraically or understand mathematical processes. With these shortcomings in mind, the members of the committee reviewed the state and national math standards, read books and journals articles, attended a national mathematics conference, tried textbooks, and visited other districts. Through this process, the committee decided that the district needed a new, and more powerful mathematics curriculum program. They selected *Everyday Math* because it was the curriculum that most closely matched the list of best practices identified in their review of the literature. Some of these best practices include a focus on thinking, problem solving and application, encouraging students to use multiple strategies to solve problems, and using multiple assessments throughout the school year. Implementing the new curriculum required intensive professional development, which is detailed in Chapter 5.

Developing a Common Language Around Good Math Instruction

As a result of the 10 teachers on the mathematics curriculum committee reading the research on math instruction and presenting it to colleagues, followed by regularly scheduled grade-level meetings where this same language was used and mathematics instruction was discussed, the district developed a common language with which to talk about math instruction. This language was based on a research-proven curriculum, and the teachers had all seen the data that proved to them that they needed to try different strategies to get their students to learn to the standards.

Summary

Several elements were critical to the dramatic improvement in student performance in mathematics at these elementary schools. First, new district leadership, with training in data-driven decision making, was an important stimulus for change in the district. Second, district teams engaged in extensive analysis of math test scores to identify where students in the district were weak in math, to help create an understanding that change was needed, to help focus the search for a new mathematics curriculum to one that focused on higher level mathematics and problem solving, and to aid the search for a new curriculum. The next important step was setting high but achievable goals—which in this case was the goal of having 90 percent of students in the district proficient or advanced in mathematics. The district then selected a new curriculum, *Everyday Math*, to specifically meet the needs of the students in this district, particularly its emphasis on problem solving and application. The district followed this initiative with extensive, new professional development and placed instructional coaches in the schools to help teachers implement the new curriculum in their classrooms, although a shortage of resources necessitated reallocating teachers from tutoring students to coaching teachers—this was a vital part of their success. As the schools implemented the new curriculum, the district restructured time during the day to provide regularly scheduled time for grade-level teams to meet and discuss mathematics instruction using the common language created by the improvement process, and shifted the focus of staff meetings to mathematics instruction, providing the necessary leadership to help shepherd the reform. Finally, the district also placed teacher-tutors in the schools to help struggling students stay with the core curriculum and learn to the expected levels. The results were more than expected: a rise in those performing at the proficient level and a more than doubling of students performing at the advanced levels.

Other Rural Examples

There undoubtedly are many other examples of rural districts restructuring and reallocating resources to produce large improvements in student performance. Sherry (2007) profiled the actions in Walsh School District in the foothills of the Rocky Mountains south of Denver. A case on the Carl Sandburg School in Freeport, Illinois, just south of the Wisconsin border and east of the Belvidere Chrysler plant in north-central Illinois, presented at the 2007 Doubling Performance Conference discussed above, provides another example of stellar performance of in a small rural district. Frankford Elementary School in rural Delaware is profiled by both Chenoweth (2007) and the Education Trust (2006) (see www.edtrust.org). Chenoweth (2007) also provides a case on the Oakland Heights Elementary School, a diverse school in rural Arkansas. Indeed, Chenoweth's book is another excellent source for cases of schools dramatically improving student performance, all existence proofs of where "it's being done"—that is, producing academic success in unexpected places and schools.

2. MEDIUM-SIZED DISTRICTS

This section includes background information on instructional improvement efforts in medium-sized districts that have doubled performance: Madison (Wisconsin), Kennewick (Washington), and two schools in medium-sized districts that have doubled performance, one in LaCrosse (Wisconsin) and one in Appleton (Wisconsin).

The Madison, Wisconsin Story[5]

Madison, Wisconsin, is a medium-sized urban district in south-central Wisconsin serving about 25,000 students. In many ways, it is like several medium-sized districts around the country. For years, it was a relatively homogeneous community with good schools and high levels of student achievement. In the late 1980s and early 1990s, its demographics began to change. By the mid-1990s it was moving past a 25 percent low-income and minority enrollment toward the 50 percent level. Today, its enrollment is 50 percent minority, quite different from the demographics of the larger community. As its diversity grew, so did the achievement gap between its middle-class, white students, and the rising numbers of low-income and minority students, particularly, African Americans.

Something had to be done. So the district conducted an equity, diversity, and adequacy "audit" of the district. This entailed an extensive analysis of state test results, including the disaggregation of the test results by various subgroups of students: low income, African American, and other minorities, as well as ELL students. It should be noted that this occurred before No Child Left Behind (NCLB). The analysis of reading achievement showed that only about 30 percent of low-income and African American students met the state's third-grade reading benchmarks, and even worse, almost all such students who scored below the basic level in reading at Grade 3 were below basic in Grade 8 as well. In other words, if students did not read at or above the basic level by Grade 3, they almost never caught up.

As a result, the district set three overarching goals for the district:

- Have all students reading at or above proficiency by the end of third grade.
- Have all students take and pass algebra by the end of Grade 9.
- Have all students take and pass geometry by the end of Grade 10.

These goals have guided the district for the past decade. These three goals—reading, algebra, and geometry—were considered "gateway" goals; if students could not meet them, they would have great difficulty exiting high school ready for college, ready for work in the global market, and ready for citizenship.

The reading goal made it clear that there was an urgent need to bolster the district's elementary reading program, actually its "nonreading" program because at that time the reading program varied by school, grade, and classroom! And it was not working for its new students.

Using a bottom-up approach that mirrored the Madison culture for any change, a group of central office experts, principals, and teachers recognized for their reading expertise created a new, districtwide, research-based reading program over a multiple-year period. In the first year, they created a short document on the nine elements of a good reading program. Teachers then asked for more detail. The document was expanded the next year, and even more detail was requested. By the end of the process, the document was quite extensive and provided explicit guidance for reading strategies that helped teachers design instructional programs each week of the school year.

During this same period, the committee also developed a document that teachers used as formative assessments to collect a "running record" of where each individual student was concerning various reading goals and objectives. The results of these running records were then discussed in groups to determine the kinds of instructional strategies they required.

Furthermore, the copies of these records were sent to a person in the central office with the responsibility to increase minority student achievement. She reviewed all records, and when she found that certain students were not making progress, she would visit the school they attended and have a meeting with the principal and teachers to determine what more could be done. The goal was to leave no child behind, as it were.

Wanting to make sure every teacher in Grades K–3 had the skills to implement the new reading and formative assessment program, the district significantly expanded professional development, ultimately providing professional development in the new reading program for all its elementary teachers, including an intensive summer induction program for all new teachers. In addition, from other resources, it provided instructional coaches for all of its highest poverty schools to help all teachers incorporate the new reading strategies into their ongoing instructional practice.

The districts also implemented two additional resource-rich strategies, funded largely by reallocating other district resources. It reduced the K–3 classrooms to 15 students in the schools that received the instructional coaches, a strategy which over time was aided by a new state policy that provided financial assistance to reduce those grade classes to the same pupil size. Second, the district also provided teacher-tutors to help students still struggling to achieve to a proficiency standard after experiencing the regular reading program.

All the new resources—professional development, instructional coaches, smaller class sizes, and teacher-tutors—were supported by reallocating the resources they had been providing to their elementary schools. No new local funds were needed.

The result was a virtual doubling over a five-year period of the percentage of low-income and African American students achieving or exceeding the proficiency level on the state's reading test, with increases of 50 percent to 78 percent and 41 percent to 69 percent, respectively. The district also reduced the number of students scoring below basic in Grade 3 to almost zero.

Summary

The core of this story is threefold: first, the setting of high expectations—all students at reading proficiency by the end of third grade; second, dramatic instructional change in the reading program by developing a districtwide reading program that all teachers were expected to implement in all classrooms; and third, focused use of resources on three evidence-based practices for the core instructional program—class sizes of 15 in Grades K–3, instructional coaches who helped teachers successfully implement new instructional approaches to reading in schools and teacher-tutors to provide intensive, extra help to students who needed it to get above basic and toward proficiency.

Another aspect of this story is the alignment of program development, which was very bottom up, and the culture of the district. Although led by skilled individuals in the central office, the program was viewed by teachers and principals in schools as a teacher-and-principal developed effort, which over time included all teachers. Furthermore, as the program matured in the primary grades, teachers in the upper-elementary grades as well as middle school teachers asked for similar assistance and attention, and the district also began to implement similar strategies for the math program.

Kennewick, Washington[6]

Kennewick, one of three midsized communities in the Tri-Cities area in southeastern Washington, provides another example of a district that has restructured its schools to achieve ambitious student achievement goals. Kennewick serves 15,000 students in 13 elementary schools,

4 middle schools, and 3 high schools. About one-fourth of its students are ethnic minorities, and about 50 percent are eligible for free and reduced-price lunch. In 1995, only 57 percent of its third-grade students read at or above the state standard for that level. The school board decided that was not good enough and, with support from the district's leaders, set the goal of educating at least 95 percent of its students to reading proficiency by the end of third grade, a goal similar to that of Madison, Wisconsin. When the federal No Child Left Behind law came along, with its ambitious Adequate Yearly Progress (AYP) goals, the district simply embraced the somewhat stiffer objectives, by viewing them as complementing and reinforcing what the district already was trying to accomplish, rather than opposing them.

At first, principals and teachers were shocked and surprised. They did not feel the goals were attainable. They had been working hard, so what else could they do?

The district, including school board members, began to lead a multiple-year awareness and professional development effort. First, the district helped each school—the principal and the entire faculty—analyze their students' test scores. In the process, each school identified several achievement gaps—the traditional one of lower-income students achieving at below-average levels but also new ones. Although differing across schools, all schools identified performance deficiencies in many subskill areas. The result was that each school became much more familiar with their performance status and the "texture" of the achievement profiles of its students, realized there was progress to be made, and became emboldened to redress many of the achievement shortcomings.

Washington Elementary is a prime example of what happened next. To begin, the school extended learning time for reading instruction, setting aside the two hours from 8:45 to 10:45 every morning for intensive reading instruction. Then, the school began to provide teachers with more professional development, both in additional summer classes and during the school year. Third, the school decided that its old reading curriculum was not good enough and adopted a new reading program from Open Court (information available at http://www.opencourtresources.com). This new reading curriculum emphasized phonemic awareness, phonics, and then comprehension—the structured approach many of the school's nonreaders needed. Fourth, during the two hours of reading instruction in the morning, the school had every staff member teach reading—core teachers; specialist art, music and PE teachers; and instructional aides. This allowed the school to have low class sizes for reading instruction. The lowest-performing readers were put into smaller classrooms and given the most expert teachers.

After a few years of implementation, when scores improved somewhat but not that much, the school decided that the students most behind needed even more instructional time if they were to catch up and read proficiently by the end of the third grade. So the school began to provide more instructional time to those students, again in small groups, during the afternoon. The students gave up some music and art instruction so they could work more at becoming a proficient reader. The theory was that reading was the cornerstone of good performance in every other subject, including mathematics.

At about the same time, the school and the district adopted the benchmark/formative testing system of the North West Evaluation Association (NWEA), a group that provides districts and schools with a Web-based diagnostic testing system that provides immediate results the next day. These assessment results were used to identify student performance in multiple reading subskills. The additional afternoon instruction was then targeted to the specific subskills students were struggling to learn. The idea here was to intervene immediately with struggling students so they learned all requisite skills as the year progressed, rather than waiting until the end of the year to see how students were performing.

Simultaneously, the school began to focus on this approach to reading at all grades. Although the most intense focus in the first couple of years had been at Grade 3, the school soon realized that hard work on reading began at kindergarten and continued through all grades. This all-grade focus, combined with the NWEA diagnostic testing and the extra help in the afternoon focused on specific reading subskills, began to accelerate achievement gains.

Throughout the entire process, the principal provided strong instructional leadership during these transformational changes. He exposed the teachers to effective reading practices, helped the faculty select a new reading textbook, and captured resources to fund ongoing professional development. During the two hours of reading instruction each morning, he would walk through all classrooms, doing "looking for" observations. He was "looking for" the eight key characteristics of the school's reading program, which gave him specific data to discuss with teachers at a later time.

The result: At Washington, reading scores jumped from having only 70 percent at third-grade proficiency in 1996 to 94 percent by 2000 and 98 percent in 2004. Although not quite as high, the district boosted the proportion of third graders reading at proficiency from 57 percent in 1995 to 88 percent in 2004, just shy of its ambitious goal of 95 percent.

Summary

The district and school recalibrated their student achievement goals, setting an ambitious goal of having at least 90 percent of students finish third-grade reading at or above proficiency for that grade. They then reengineered the school schedule to provide two hours of reading instruction to all students every morning, reduced class sizes by having all teachers— including music and PE teachers—teach reading during that time, and provided the best teachers to the lowest-performing reading group. Teachers also engaged in ongoing diagnostic testing of their students so they knew exactly what each student did and did not know and could then target instruction to subskills needing more attention. The school also replaced the old reading program with a brand-new reading program, more structured and more relevant to the learning needs of its students. They redesigned the teacher development system, by helping teachers to engage in detailed and sophisticated ongoing formative assessment of their students and by providing additional professional development on more effective reading strategies both during the summer and at different points throughout the school year. They relentlessly pursued the goal of having all their struggling students achieve by providing additional and targeted instruction during the afternoon to all students struggling to learn to proficiency. The schools that made the most progress were led by individuals who aggressively engaged in instructional leadership.

LaCrosse, Wisconsin[7]

Franklin Elementary is a welcoming place where learning is emphasized, valued, and reinforced. It is one of 10 elementary schools in the school district of La Crosse, Wisconsin, which served approximately 7,200 students during the 2005–2006 school year. Franklin is a small school with 235 students, 44 percent of whom are minority (30 percent Hmong, many with ELL needs), 69 percent participate in the free or reduced-price lunch program, and 9 percent qualify for special education services. By comparison, the student population in the district is 20 percent minority, 36 percent low-income (as indicated by participation in free or reduced-price lunch), and 12 percent special education. Working under the enthusiastic leadership of a new principal with high expectations for teachers and students alike, dedicated teachers at Franklin have raised student test scores.

Improving Test Scores in the School

Between 2002 and 2005, fourth graders at Franklin posted dramatically higher scores on the math portion of the Wisconsin state tests (see Table 1.2). For all students as a group, scores went from 23 percent proficient in 2002 to 77 percent proficient in 2005—the scores more than tripled! There was also impressive growth in the percentage of students who scored at the advanced level in mathematics during that time. In

Table 1.2   Franklin's Improving Test Scores

NOTE: WKCE = Wisconsin Knowledge and Concepts Examinations.

2002, only 10 percent of students scored at the advanced level, compared to 31 percent in 2005—again, a tripling of scores. In reading, fourth-grade test scores rose from 57 percent proficient in 2002 to a high of 87 percent in 2003, falling slightly in 2006 to 85 percent and then to 77 percent in 2005. Although some of the gains were not sustained, reading scores still improved by 20 percentage points during the time period in question.

School Improvement Process

The growth in achievement at Franklin is the result of the collaborative effort of education professionals committed to improving student learning. From strong leadership at the district level to a dedicated principal with a site leadership team and a group of dedicated teachers, all of these elements contributed to the success. But the process took time. When the new principal arrived in 1999, he saw some dynamics that he believed needed to be addressed, such as teachers having low expectations for some students. Knowing that it would take some time to build his influence as a leader, he began by talking about high expectations. Some teachers were not as receptive as others to the new mantra, and over the next few years, 10 employees (teachers, teaching assistants, media specialists) who no longer fit in, left the school. Over time, the combination of strong principal leadership and the assembling of a group of teachers devoted to helping students learn have led to continued success in raising student test scores.

Gaining a Principal Who Was a True Instructional Leader

The principal at Franklin knew that having effective teachers in the classroom was the best way to ensure that students learned as much as possible. For this reason, he tried to protect time on task (two hours for reading and one for math each day) and was careful not to take the expert teachers out of the classroom too often. He was strategic about who was hired at Franklin—the prospective employee had to be willing and able to meet the high expectations for teaching and learning that he set. He also tried to be in the classroom as much as possible.

Site Team Helps Lead the School

The principal cited the support and vision of the site leadership team as critical to helping maintain momentum in a positive direction. Placing teachers in leadership roles allowed them to influence more of the staff to continue to improve instruction.

Leadership and Support From the District

The principal also attributed some of the school's success to the leadership and support he received from the central office. Some examples include a districtwide reading program and annual formative reading assessment, a district writing program, and an annual data-driven retreat for site leadership teams from each school.

Meeting the Challenge of Powerful Curricular Materials

In 1999, Franklin adopted a new math series called Math Investigations (information available at http://investigations.terc.edu/). When the test scores were low, some teachers complained that the test did not seem to be measuring what they were teaching. The principal and site team recognized that this was an instructional issue and helped ensure that teachers received the help they needed to improve their mathematics instruction.

Professional Development

The principal altered the school schedule to build in time for collaboration whenever possible and used professional development days for teachers to meet across grade levels. Having time to collaborate around instruction helped to build community and further helped teachers to improve teaching in their own classrooms. Franklin also had a mentor program in place to provide new teachers the additional professional development needed at the beginning of a teaching career, including visiting other classrooms to observe expert teachers in action.

Multiple Strategies for Struggling Students

As in many U.S. schools, when differentiated instruction is necessary in a classroom, aides often teach one group of students. At Franklin, rather than putting the instructional aide with the students struggling most, the aide now works with the students who need the least help, freeing teachers to use their expertise where it was most desperately needed. It also helped that Franklin was one of the original SAGE[8] schools, so class sizes were 15 or below in Grades K–3, which allowed struggling students to get more attention from their teachers. In 2000, Franklin began offering an after-school program and recently added a before-school program to help support students and families with less-flexible work schedules. Franklin also offered summer school with instruction in reading and math for four weeks and enrichment activities for an additional five weeks. Although instruction in core courses is what helps raise test scores, extending the summer session by five weeks helped ensure that children who needed school food to meet their nutritional needs are at school most of the summer.

Districtwide Formative Reading Assessment Gauges Progress and Early Problems

Because the state standardized tests that the students took each year did not give information in a timely manner, the district implemented its own reading assessment. Each child took the district test in the fall, and results were shared with students, parents, and teachers, which allowed time for teachers to concentrate their work with students in the areas identified as needing improvement. The principal and teacher leaders recognized that students who did not leave first grade knowing how to read tended to get behind and never catch up, so they were very vigilant with that age group.

An Emphasis on Writing

Citing research that writing helps boost all scores, the principal emphasized the importance of writing by quarterly requiring teachers to submit writing samples for each student. This was another means of identifying students in need of extra help and another source of information that teachers used in the classroom.

A Welcoming School Community

The principal and the teachers made multiple efforts to create a welcoming environment for parents, students, and school employees. One way this was done was to choose a theme each year with activities all year and a program for parents at the end of the year. As a result, parents trusted the staff, the PTO was very active, and both the school and the community felt supported.

Extensive Programming to Maximize Parent Involvement

Programs that involved parents included an at-home program called Reading: A Family Affair to involve parents in reading and a program called Mother Read, Father Read that met after school for eight weeks to provide literacy instruction for both students and their parents. The school also produced a video about classroom management procedures and how the school operated so that parents who could not physically be in school were connected and knew what to expect. School leaders also involved parents by soliciting their opinions every other year to find out how they could serve them better.

Summary

Several elements were critical to the dramatic improvement in Franklin's scores. The first included strong leadership from the principal who set high expectations for all students. The improvement process at Franklin began when a new principal was hired, a principal who was willing to start the conversation about the need for high expectations for all students and make it clear that those who were not able to meet the challenge of expecting more from all kids (and also from themselves) would no longer fit in at the school. The second was an explicit focus on improving the mathematics and language arts—reading and writing—programs. New programs were adopted, and teachers were provided extensive professional development. These were bolstered by adoption of formative assessments for reading so teachers could tailor their instruction to the exact needs of the students in their own classrooms. Third, the school provided multiple extra supports for struggling students. From providing before- and afterschool programs and summer school to having certified teachers (rather than instructional aides) work with students in need of extra help, Franklin prioritized the learning needs of those in danger of falling behind to maximize their chance of success, thus relentlessly working to get all students up to and beyond proficiency. Fourth, with additional state funds, the school was able to lower class sizes in Grades K–3 to just 15 students. Fifth, the principal was supported by a strong site team, which was called the principal's closest team of advisors, and cited their vision and positive thinking as essential to the school's continued success. District leaders helped place needed emphasis on core areas in many ways, including administering a formative assessment in reading each fall and distributing the results in a timely manner and convening an annual data-driven retreat for site teams to analyze their school's data. Finally, the principal and teachers worked hard to make the school an inviting place for students and parents, including hosting numerous activities that parents and students attended together and offering programs that helped parents stay involved at home too, particularly with literacy.

Columbus School in Appleton, Wisconsin[9]

Columbus Elementary is one of 16 elementary schools in the Appleton School District in east-central Wisconsin's Fox River Valley. Appleton is home to 77,000 residents, approximately 15,000 of whom are students attending Appleton's 23 public and 12 charter schools. The students in this district are primarily white (81% in 2005–2006), but the minority population is growing—in 1995–1996, 89 percent of students were white. The largest minority group (10 percent) is Asian; Appleton is one of a number of cities in Wisconsin with a sizable Hmong population. The next largest is Hispanic, at 5 percent. Columbus Elementary has 174 students, who as a group, are more racially and economically diverse than the district as a whole. Approximately 57 percent of Columbus's students are white, 26 percent are Asian (Hmong), 8 percent are black, 6 percent are Hispanic, and 3 percent are American Indian. Of the school's Hmong students, 14 percent are ELL. Districtwide, 28 percent of students qualify for free or reduced-price lunch; at Columbus, 73 percent are eligible.

Improving Test Scores in the School

In 1999, only 49 percent of the fourth-grade students at Columbus Elementary scored at the advanced or proficient level on the reading portion of the Wisconsin state test, and only 45 percent were advanced or proficient in math. The school received notice that it was in danger of being declared a school in need of improvement. A new principal was hired for the 1998–1999 school year after the former principal retired. The new principal initiated a needs assessment with the help of the Wisconsin Department of Public Instruction (WDPI) to help identify the specific issues on which the school needed to work. Over the next six years, a combination of factors, some set in motion by the needs assessment and some a result of district, state, and federal policies, led to dramatic improvement in test scores at Columbus Elementary.

Although the scores on the state test before 2002 cannot be directly compared with the scores post-2002, comparing the scores between 2002 and 2005 shows a large improvement in both reading and math. As Figure 1.3 illustrates, progress on reading scores has been a steady upward trajectory, moving from 51 percent of students advanced or proficient in 2002 to 90 percent in 2005. Fourth-grade math scores have also increased from 55 percent in 2002 to 75 percent in 2005, but as Figure 1.3 shows, scores were even higher in 2003 and 2004 than they were in 2005. However, as Figure 1.4 illustrates, the percentage of fourth-grade students scoring at the advanced level in math had a more consistently positive trajectory, moving from 17 percent in 2002 to 30 percent in 2005. The most dramatic increase of all is also illustrated in Figure 1.4, and that is the growth in the percentage

Figure 1.3   Improving Test Scores at Columbus

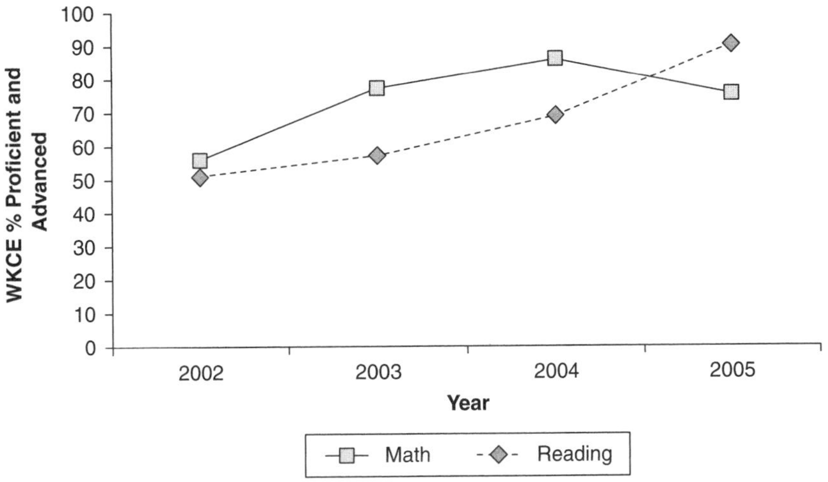

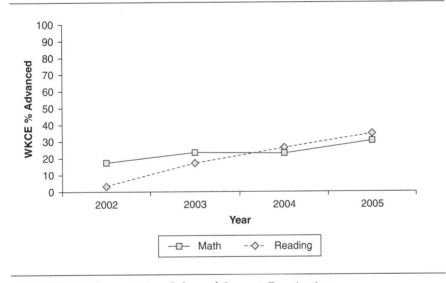

NOTE: WKCE = Wisconsin Knowledge and Concepts Examinations.

Figure 1.4   Growth in Students Scoring Advanced

NOTE: WKCE = Wisconsin Knowledge and Concepts Examinations.

of Columbus students scoring at the advanced level in reading. In 2002, only 3 percent scored at the advanced level, and by 2005, that percentage had increased more than tenfold to 35 percent!

Columbus School Improvement Process

For Columbus Elementary, the combination of the fear of being labeled a school in need of improvement and the vigor of the new principal set in motion a process that would turn the school around. When the new principal learned that the school was in danger of being labeled a school in need of improvement, she contacted WDPI for assistance with a needs assessment. She and a district administrator worked with WDPI to analyze the school's test score data and the alignment of its curriculum with state standards. This process identified the following five needs:

1. Coordinate existing programs and resources to maximize student learning.

2. Revise the school schedule to maximize instructional time.

3. Link assessment to instruction—students will not be able to perform well on a test if they are not taught the material the test covers.

4. Have higher expectations of all students and their ability to develop higher-order thinking skills.

5. Coordinate staff development so that it is linked to what teachers need to improve instruction.

To accomplish these tasks, the principal decided the school would need transformational resources. She applied for a comprehensive school reform grant in January of 1999, and the grant was awarded in July of that same year. This grant provided the school with an additional $75,000 per year, renewable for up to three years, conditional on the selection and successful implementation of a comprehensive school reform program.

The school adopted several other programmatic changes. It became a SAGE school, which provided the resources to reduce class sizes in Grades K–3 to 15 students; it became a 21st-century school, which provided the resources to offer an afterschool program staffed with certified teacher-tutors; it obtained additional funding to hire certified teacher-tutors to work after school with homeless students; and it built formative assessments into the school year so that students in need of extra help were identified early.

Choosing a Comprehensive School Design With a New Curriculum Program Combined With Extensive Staff Development

The school knew it needed more than structural and programmatic changes; it also need an instructional and curriculum program tailored to the needs of its students. So the staff searched for a comprehensive instructional program that would help them address the needs of the ELL while also changing the attitudes and skills of the teachers responsible for teaching these and other more challenging students. The staff reviewed different designs and selected Different Ways of Knowing (DWOK), a product of the Galef Institute that had proved to be successful with students who were ELL.

The principal cited the staff development that accompanied the design as being key to transforming both the expectations for students and their instructional methods. Chapter 5 provides more details on the professional development program, and Chapter 6 details the multiple supports for struggling students the school implemented.

Developing and Maintaining a Professional School Community

The atmosphere created by the process of collaboratively undergoing a needs assessment, researching different school designs, and selecting a design as the school's new instructional approach created a sense of unity among the staff at Columbus that developed into a professional community over time. The selection of Different Ways of Knowing and all of the professional development that it involved, in particular the days on-site with the same coach, helped build an atmosphere of openness in the school. The coach encouraged teachers to spend time in each others' classrooms, learning from and helping each other, and the comprehensive school reform grant provided the extra funding that enabled teachers to get substitutes so that they could be observers in each others' classrooms. The knowledge and skills that the teachers gained from the staff at the Galef Institute helped build their sense of efficacy with all students, particularly the ELL and other struggling students with whom they had not been as successful in the past. When test scores began to rise, teachers were further buoyed, which renewed their commitment to helping all children learn.

Successfully Involving Parents in Their Students' Education

The school redoubled efforts to involve parents during the comprehensive school reform process. For example, they offered parenting courses while providing dinner and child care, which helped parents feel more a part of the school community. Another way that the principal helped parents feel comfortable was to have the necessary translators on staff so that parents could communicate with the school. Finally, providing resources such as Math-at-Home (a program where backpacks, available for checkout, contain manipulatives, flashcards, measuring tools, and other learning materials that parents can use to help reinforce what students learn at school) gave parents the necessary tools to reinforce at home what students were learning at school.

Strong, Ingenuous Leadership to Guide the Process

A key element of the school's success was the leadership provided by the principal, hired just as the school was being placed on a list of schools in danger of being labeled in need of improvement. Her we-can-do-it attitude helped inspire staff, and her tireless efforts to obtain additional funding made many of the important changes at Columbus possible.

Summary

The success of administrators, teachers, and students at Columbus Elementary was the result of a combination of factors. First, they used data to determine what improvements were most important. The needs assessment allowed the new principal to focus her efforts on what was most urgently needed: changes in both the instructional program and staff expectations so that students could learn the skills they needed to perform well on standardized tests.

Second, they raised the expectations for all students regardless of background. To accomplish the goal, Columbus teachers needed a new way to teach students who did not know English, and they set high expectations for the learning of all the students in their school, regardless of the conditions that made learning difficult.

Third, the school adopted a new curriculum and teaching philosophy to meet the needs of the student body. The selection of Different Ways of Knowing allowed the school to use the new curriculums selected by the district (Harcourt for literacy and Houghton Mifflin for math) while bringing the high expectations and methods that helped their students succeed with the thinking, problem solving, and application aspects of that curriculum.

Fourth, the school invested heavily in new and intensive professional development. The prior experience of the principal told her that to change how teachers taught, extensive staff development was needed. The comprehensive school reform grant was critical in providing the resources necessary to allow teachers to see the new method of instruction demonstrated, practice it in their own classrooms, and conduct and receive formative evaluations from peers and consultants—the kind of professional development that leads to instructional change.

Fifth, the school made additional structural changes. For one, it lowered class sizes in the early grades with the help of a state grant, though under different leadership the school had previously turned away those funds because of a "lack of space." Knowing the critical importance of smaller class sizes to learning in the early grades, the new principal found a way to lower class sizes by renting space from the building across the street. As a result, the school had classrooms of 15 or fewer students in Grades K–3.

Sixth, the school built informative assessments to identify where each student was and to target struggling students with extra help early. The principal attributed much of the school's success in literacy to the use of running records, which allowed teachers to identify what students knew and what they still needed to learn, enabling teachers to be much more efficient in their instruction. They did not need to spend time reviewing material students already knew and could spend more time in areas where students were weaker. They could also refer students for extra help when they needed more than could be provided in the classroom.

Seventh, the school provided a variety of extra-help strategies to support struggling students. Providing support to students from low-income backgrounds is essential to their success and to the success of any struggling student. At Columbus, multiple supports were in place, including a program for first graders called United for Reading Success (URS), where volunteers trained by the district work one-on-one with students struggling to learn to read. Columbus also offered an afterschool program staffed with two certified teachers to tutor students for one hour, with additional certified teacher-tutors to work with homeless students. The school also has a reading specialist to help students during the school day who need small-group or one-on-one instruction.

Eighth, from all these actions working together as a faculty with the principal, the school created an atmosphere of collaborative decision making and professional community. The principal knew the importance of involving multiple staff members in any training or leadership opportunity she was offered. She purposely took a different teacher with her each time she traveled to either state or district professional development or to programs offered by the Galef Institute. This allowed information to flow horizontally through the school, from one teacher to another, rather than just vertically, from administration to staff.

Finally, the school involved parents and the community. The staff at Columbus knew that it was vital to the success of their students to have parents partner with the school to support student learning.

3. DOUBLING PERFORMANCE IN HIGH-MINORITY, HIGH-POVERTY SCHOOLS

This section includes cases on Reading First Schools in Washington, schools with very high concentrations of poverty, minority, and ELL students, which are characteristic of many low-performing schools in many large urban districts. The section also includes a summary of instructional improvement efforts at Victory School in Milwaukee, Wisconsin. Since our school's finance adequacy work, including research on schools and districts doubling performance, has been conducted during the past four years in Arkansas, Wyoming, Washington, and Wisconsin, most of our examples derive from those states. But there is a large complementary literature of cases of schools in large urban districts as well as large, urban districts themselves producing large gains in student academic learning and a closing of the achievement gap. Readers are encouraged to read the following cases:

- Elmont Junior/Senior High School, a school of nearly 2,000 students, almost all minority and mostly African American, which has consistently produced top student performance and is one of the best high schools in New York State. Cases are provided by both Chenoweth (2007) and the Education Trust (2006).

- Baltimore Talent Development High School, a predominately low-income and African American high school in Baltimore and Dayton's Bluff Elementary school, an all-poverty and 50-percent-minority school in St. Paul, Minnesota, presented at the 2007 Wisconsin Conference on Doubling Performance (see www.education.wisc.edu/elpa/conferences/WILA/). Dayton's Bluff also is profiled in Chenoweth (2007).

- Chenoweth (2007) also provides a case of Centennial Elementary School in Atlanta, the Benbow Initiative for the Chattanooga Public Schools, while the Education Trust (2006) profiles Capital View Elementary School in the same district.

- Supovitz's (2006) extensive analysis of dramatic improvement in Duvall County, Jacksonville, Florida is an excellent example of districtwide improvement.

- Finally, Mary Hall Stanton Elementary in Philadelphia changed from one of the lowest-performing Philadelphia schools to one of the highest-performing schools in the state of Pennsylvania under the leadership of principal Barbara Adderly, according to another case by the Education Trust (2006) (www.edtrust.org).

Other examples of districts that have produced systemwide, dramatic improvement include Aldine, Texas (profiled by the Education Trust, 2006), Long Beach and Garden Grove, California, both profiled by the Broad Foundation, and the Zone Schools in Miami-Dade County, Florida.

In summation, in addition to our cases, there are several other cases in the literature that describe how schools in large urban districts as well as districts themselves have dramatically improved performance and closed the achievement gap.

Reading First Schools in Washington State

We first profile the Washington State Reading First initiative, which focuses not only on students in kindergarten through Grade 3 but also schools with the highest concentrations of low income, minority, and ELL students—that is, elementary schools that present the toughest education challenges. The goal of the Reading First program, in Washington as well as across the country, was to produce students who read at or above grade level by the end of third grade. The core of the Reading First process is a scientific, research-based reading program; schools are able to select one program from a menu of programs that have been documented through rigorous research to produce reading proficiency. As you could glean from the examples we have already shared in this chapter, any educational initiative that is designed to impact student academic achievement reflected in scores on state student achievement tests, must begin as a curriculum and instructional initiative. Designers of the federal Reading First program claim—validly from our perspective—that the country has sufficient professional knowledge to insure that all students exit third grade with proficiency in reading in English.[10]

The Washington Reading First process takes a systemic, district approach. The K–3 comprehensive reading programs used by the schools in the program align with the state's standards in reading and provide detailed instructional advice to all staff involved in daily reading instruction, including teachers and paraprofessionals. The reading curriculum is the foundation of the Reading First program.

An additional key component of the Reading First process is the development of a comprehensive assessment system. This system includes screening, progress monitoring, and diagnostic and program assessments. Program or "formative" assessments are commonly linked to the state's reading test but provide more detailed data to teachers on the exact knowledge, skills, and understandings of students in reading at each, different grade level. These assessments are then used as guides by teachers who identify specific reading objectives and deploy explicit instructional strategies that are linked both to the state and district reading standards and to the status of the individual teachers' students' reading proficiency levels. This intense classroom focus is then bolstered by a district-level reading coordinator, reading coaches in all Reading First elementary schools, and two tiers of intensive intervention for struggling students. These interventions include very small group tutoring provided by teacher-tutors or trained and supervised paraprofessionals. The Reading First process is then embedded within a school that hopefully is designed to reflect the nine research-based elements of effective schools.

In K–3 Reading First classrooms, students receive 90 minutes of uninterrupted reading instruction daily. This day-to-day instructional treatment, of course, is the core of the program. And if implemented well, it should educate the bulk of K–3 students—including low-income and minority students—to reading proficiency in English by the end of third grade. To ensure that all staff providing reading instruction and interventions

Table 1.3   Student Performance Outcomes in Washington's 51 Reading First
Elementary Schools

Performance Standard	Percentage of Students at This Level in 1997	Percentage of Students at This Level in 2003	Percentage of Students at This Level in 2005
Below basic	26	17	11
Basic	43	42	25
Proficient, met standard	19	32	45
Exceeded proficiency standard	6	8	18

(including teachers and paraprofessionals) have the instructional expertise and capacity to deliver high-powered reading instruction, Reading First includes intensive professional development each year for its subgrantees, detailed in Chapter 5. Reading First also includes several strategies for struggling students described in Chapter 6.

The program has produced remarkable results. It should be noted that most Washington Reading First schools have large numbers of students from low-income and minority backgrounds, so present the toughest educational challenges. Producing performance gains in these schools, which have had the lowest levels of student academic achievement, is critical if Washington is to produce students capable of working in the knowledge-based and high-skilled economy of the 21st century. Table 1.3 summarizes the outcomes.

Washington Reading First was introduced to these schools in 2003. The numbers show that although the schools had been making some progress over the six years from 1997–2003, the Reading First intervention dramatically accelerated the progress. The percentage of students scoring below the basic level declined by nine points (1.5 points a year) over the six years from 1997–2003 but then declined by six points (three points per year) in the first two years of Reading First, or double the previous trend. Similarly, although the percentage scoring at the proficient level rose from 19 percent to 32 percent in the six years from 1997–2003 (13 points or about two points a year), that percentage accelerated after 2003, rising by the same total amount (13 points) but at three times the annual rate (6 points a year) compared to the previous trend. And finally, the percentage scoring at or above proficient or standard rose by 15 points from 25 percent to 40 percent from 1997–2003 but then jumped by 23 points to 63 percent in just two years from 2003–2005. The data showed that gains similar to these were made in the Reading First schools by all minority subgroups—African Americans, Hispanics, and Native Americans. These significant results—on the state testing system—show that the Washington Reading First program is an outcome-oriented strategy that weaves together a set of resources to produce student achievement results.

Victory School in Milwaukee, Wisconsin[11]

Victory School is a self-proclaimed "gifted and talented" school, but students need not pass any sort of entrance exam. Instead, the school promises to take children at nearly any level and move them from wherever they begin to as far as they can go. Victory is a K–8 school in the Milwaukee Public School District, a large urban district with about 93,000 students in 227 schools. The district serves significant low-income and minority populations; in 2005–2006, the student body was 55 percent black, 22 percent Hispanic, 18 percent white, 5 percent Asian, and 1 percent American Indian. Districtwide, 74 percent of students are eligible for free or reduced-price lunch; among elementary students, the count is higher, at 80 percent. The demographics at Victory are not quite as poor and not as heavily minority; in 2005–2006, 68 percent of students qualified for subsidized lunch, and 44 percent of students were white, 26 percent were Hispanic, 25 percent black, 5 percent Asian, and 1 percent American Indian. With a dedicated leadership team, support from the district, and consistently high expectations, the test scores at Victory have risen dramatically in the last five years.

Improving Test Scores at Victory

In November of 2002, only 20 percent of students at Victory scored at the advanced or proficient level in math, while 62 percent scored at these levels in reading. Because low achievement plagued much of the district, district leaders initiated a number of reforms that helped boost achievement at Victory. As Figure 1.5 illustrates, between 2002 and 2005, the percentage of fourth-grade students achieving at the advanced or proficient level in math more than tripled, moving from 20 percent to 66 percent! Fourth-grade reading scores improved modestly between 2002 and 2005, although scores fell between 2002 and 2003. Beginning at 62 percent in 2002, by 2005, they were up to 79 percent at the advanced and proficient level.

Figure 1.5 Improvements in Fourth-Grade Math and Reading at Victory

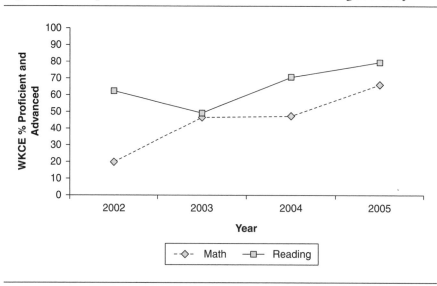

NOTE: WKCE = Wisconsin Knowledge and Concepts Examinations.

A slightly different picture emerges when the improvement in test scores is viewed not through the lens of the percentage of students achieving at the advanced and proficient level, as illustrated in Figure 1.5, but by focusing on the improvement in the percentage of students achieving at the advanced level. As illustrated in Figure 1.6, between 2002 and 2005, the percentage of students scoring at the advanced level more than doubled in reading, going from 10 percent to 24 percent. Furthermore, whereas the trajectory for reading shown in Figure 1.5 goes down between the first two years and then rises over the last two, the trajectory in Figure 1.6 is quite different; the percentage of students scoring at the advanced level rises steadily for the first three years and then drops. For example, whereas the trajectory for fourth-grade reading scores goes down between 2002 and 2003 in Figure 1.5, in Figure 1.6, it rises steadily for the first three years and then falls in the fourth year.

Like the math gains shown in Figure 1.5, Figure 1.6 demonstrates the dramatic gains in the percentage of fourth-grade students scoring at the advanced level in math, moving from 3 percent in 2002 to 24 percent in 2006!

Victory School's Improvement Process

From its inception, Victory School was a place with high expectations for its students. Formerly an only elementary school, when the school slowly became a K–8 school by adding a grade each year, school leaders

Figure 1.6   Doubling Performance at Advanced Level

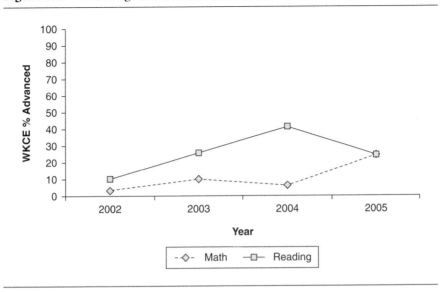

NOTE: WKCE = Wisconsin Knowledge and Concepts Examinations.

were careful to hire teachers who fit into the culture of high expectations that already existed at the school. The story of how and why test scores rose at Victory is very much a story of how standards-based reform and NCLB changed district policy, which in turn brought changes to the school level.

District Sets Clear Goals for Learning

In the 2002–2003 school year, Milwaukee Public Schools created Learning Targets to help schools understand how Wisconsin's Model Academic Standards, which at the time only existed for Grades 4, 8, and 12, could be translated down to the other grade levels. These learning targets were written and disseminated in multiple ways—one version was distributed to parents, another made into posters for teachers to display in their classrooms—which helped get everyone to have shared expectations for learning at each grade level. Teachers were then expected to show in their education plans how they incorporated the standards into their teaching. At Victory, teachers embraced this process and were supported by the school-level support positions described below.

District Implements More School-Level Support Positions

Then, the Milwaukee public schools added a position called Implementer at school sites, much like a curriculum director but also the person to handle the assessments and to see the big picture of what was needed for teachers to be successful teaching students to high standards. Shortly thereafter, other positions to help support the staff were added, including a literacy coach and a math teacher leader. The implementer, coaches, and literacy and math teacher leaders were instrumental over time in helping teachers change their practice to incorporate the standards.

Formative Assessments Help Struggling Students Get Help When They Need It

The district also implemented a system where students were tested on classroom assessments based on standards. The Student Promotion System (SPS) is the official recording program of proficiency data for Milwaukee public schools. The SPS generates reports for students in Grades K–8 and informs parents about how their child is progressing at a particular grade level on classroom assessments based on standards. This system helps identify students who need help as well as teachers who may need help to improve their instruction on a particular topic.

Distributed Leadership Team at the School Level Maintains Focus on Instruction

The position of principal at Victory changed hands a number of times, making the role of the school leadership team (officially called the Learning Team) critical to its success. The Learning Team was composed of the implementer, the coaches, and a teacher from each grade level. This group met two times per month to work on the school's education plan and to plan events focused around instruction that also builds community.

School-Level Professional Community Emphasized and Fostered

The leadership team has implemented another important program: collaborative professional development time for teachers. These meetings, 12 hours in total spread throughout the year, each have a particular instructional focus and give time for teachers to learn from each other while building community.

Involvement in Gifted and Talented Network Generates Ideas

Through professional development with an educational consultant from the South Milwaukee School District who specializes in gifted and talented students and schools, Victory school leaders learned more about the characteristics of gifted children and ways of providing challenging learning for all students. A video showed ways of challenging gifted students in the regular classroom. The learning team walked away with three gifted education models that did not cost extra money: namely, differentiation, cluster grouping, and acceleration.

Enrichment Opportunities Offered to Students

Students at Victory school have multiple opportunities for enrichment. One of these is called Creative Sharp, a literacy program for students in Grades 2–5, designed to increase reading and writing levels of grade-school students through exposure to art and history. The premise of the program is that students achieve more in their education by interacting with the visual arts and art history as part of their daily curriculum. Another example is the Dr. Martin Luther King, Jr. Writing Contest, in which the whole school participates, at different levels, in writing focused on this topic.

Victory is also the site of the country's first Italian Immersion program—one of the four-year-old kindergarten classrooms is taught exclusively in Italian.

Summary

The dramatic growth in student achievement at Victory is the result of a confluence of factors that are summarized below:

1. *Maintain high expectations for all students regardless of background.* One of the keys to the success of Victory is that it is a self-described gifted and talented school, which does not mean that students must take a test to be admitted but means that the school staff believes all students are gifted and talented, so the school provides special, often schoolwide opportunities for students to showcase their talents.

2. *Align curriculum with district and state standards and ensure that teachers know what students need to learn.* Milwaukee public schools helped teachers focus on what students need to know. They published learning targets for every subject, every grade, and teachers must post the targets and distribute informational brochures to parents so that everyone understands what is expected of students at various grade levels in every subject.

3. *Lower class sizes in the early grades.* Victory benefits from the SAGE program, Wisconsin's class-size reduction program for schools serving students in poverty. As a result, they are able to provide students with classrooms of 15 or fewer classmates, a research-proven strategy for boosting achievement, particularly for minorities and low-income students.

4. *Build in multiple (including formative) assessments to ensure struggling students get help early.* Victory used a district-initiated system called SPS, which stands for student promotion system. The SPS report is intended to

be informational at Grades K, 1, 2, 3, 5, 6, and 7. It informs the parents as to the expected grade-level progress and provides the teacher with the opportunity to monitor progress and intervene when necessary to provide support to students who perform below grade-level expectations. (At Grades 4 and 8, the report is the basis for promotion.) The school also uses running records for literacy in Grades K–3.

5. *Provide extra help to struggling students and teachers.* When students are identified as in need of extra help, they receive more one-on-one or small-group instruction, sometimes with a paraeducator and sometimes with the literacy or math specialist in the school. These specialists also serve in a coaching capacity when teachers need additional support, by working directly with the teacher by modeling classroom lessons.

6. *Distribute leadership to those willing to meet regularly and focus on learning.* The Learning Team at Victory, composed of nine teachers and the school's program implementer, has been critical to its success, by taking part in such important decisions as hiring new staff and continually working on the school's education plan, which reflects how the school plans to meet the challenges of state and district standards and national accountability. Although the principalship has changed hands numerous times, the consistency of the learning team has helped keep the school progressing forward.

7. *Provide collaborative planning time for teachers and ensure that the focus of this time is instruction.* Both the principal and the implementer spoke about the importance of providing this bimonthly time for teachers to collaborate around instruction. Teachers take turns bringing examples of student work, discussing it, scoring it, and talking about how to teach for understanding at all levels.

8. *Support students and families by extending the school day.* Victory provides a before- and afterschool program, funded by a 21st-century schools grant. The afterschool program gives students an opportunity to get help on homework from a paraeducator.

SUMMARY

These examples of schools and districts that have dramatically improved student achievement, summarized in Tables 1.4 and 1.5, share a number of common themes. First, in every case the instructional improvement was part of a large-scale change process and at least in part, a response to NCLB and/or state standards-based reform. Both of these issues are discussed in the next chapter. In the following chapter, all of the themes from this chapter are boiled down to 10 steps for doubling performance.

Table 1.4   Districts That Doubled Performance

Districts	State	Locale or Size	Percentage FRL[a]	Math Increase[b]	Reading Increase[b]	Main Features
Rosalia	WA	Rural	50	43 to 85	32 to 94	Data; set high goals; PD[c]; small reading classes; ED[d]
Abbotsford	WI	Rural	62	55 to 87	79 to 94	Guided reading; PD[c]; data; small classes K–3; tutors
Monroe	WI	Rural	23	75 to 87	N/A	Data; *Everyday Math*; PD[c]; set goals; coaches; tutors
Madison	WI	Medium	50	N/A	50 to 75 (low income)	Small classes K–3; high goals; tutors; coaches; data; PD[c]
Kennewick	WA	Medium	50	N/A	57 to 88	Data; set high goals; literacy block; Open Court; PD[c]

a. FRL refers to free and reduced-price lunches

b. See text for data on additional subgroups and grades.

c. PD refers to professional development

d. ED refers to extended-day programs.

Table 1.5   Schools That Doubled Performance

Schools	State	District	Percentage FRL[a]	Math Increase Percentage[b]	Reading Increase Percentage[b]	Main Features
Northside Elementary	WI	Monroe	23	29 to 66 (adv)	N/A	See Monroe above
Parkside Elementary	WI	Monroe	23	25 to 61 (adv)	N/A	See Monroe above
Washington Elementary	WA	Kennewick	50	N/A	70 to 98	See Kennewick above
Franklin Elementary	WI	LaCrosse	69	23 to 77	57 to 87	High expectations; Math Investigations; PD[c]; small classes K–3; data
Columbus Elementary	WI	Appleton	73	55 to 75	51 to 90	High expectations; data; Different Ways of Knowing; PD[c]
Victory K–8	WI	Milwaukee	68	20 to 66	62 to 79	Data; coaches; high expectations; small classes K–3; PD[c]; ED[d]

a. FRL refers to free and reduced-price lunches.

b. See text for data on additional subgroups and grades.

c. PD refers to professional development.

d. ED refers to extended-day programs.

NOTES

1. We also realize that all state tests are not the "best" measurements of student achievement, and that more performance-oriented tests would measure a broader range of student learning. We encourage states and districts to use more comprehensive testing systems over time but accept the fact that doubling performance on current state tests still represents major, substantive improvements in student performance.

2. Adapted from a case in Fermanich et al. (2006).

3. This case was adapted from a case in Odden, Picus, Archibald, et al. 2007).

4. This case was researched and written by Sarah Archibald.

5. This case is adapted from Odden, Picus, Archibald, et al. (2007). See also the Madison presentation at the 2007 Wisconsin Doubling Performance Conference at www.education.wisc.edu/elpa/conferences/WILA/.

6. Derived from information in Fielding, Kerr, and Rosier (2004). See also the Kennewick presentation at the 2007 Wisconsin Doubling Performance Conference at www.education.wisc.edu/elpa/conferences/WILA/.

7. This case was adapted from Odden, Picus, and Archibald et al. (2007).

8. SAGE is a state program that provides districts about $2,000 per Title I–eligible student in Grades K–3 if the school commits to lowering class size in those grades to 15 students.

9. This case was adapted from Odden, Picus, and Archibald et al. (2007). See also the Appleton presentation at the 2007 Wisconsin Doubling Performance Conference at www.education.wisc.edu/elpa/conferences/WILA/.

10. We are aware of the controversies and problems surrounding the federal management of the Reading First program; those problems do not, however, erode the impressive accomplishments of these Washington schools.

11. This case was adapted from Odden, Picus, Archibald, Goetz, Aportela, & Mangan (2007).

The Stimulus for Change and the Educational Change Process

I t is clear that the public, policymakers, parents, the business community, and most educators want large improvements in public education. We often are asked what it takes to get the education system focused on an agenda of improving student performance. The kinds of questions asked include the following: Why do schools or districts begin the process to double performance? What triggers or stimulates places to take on these achievement challenges? What can we do to focus the district and each school concerning the need to increase student performance overall and close the achievement gap?

We also are asked about the change process involved in responding to these performance pressures. Do we know anything about such large-scale organizational change? What does it look like in the private sector, and is public education all that different?

Chapters 2 and 3 address these issues. Section 1 of this chapter summarizes the pressures that moved the schools and districts profiled in Chapter 1 to begin the process of dramatically improving student learning as well as the schools and districts in the first edition of the book to restructure and reallocate resources. Section 2 gives more information about the large-scale change process.

The fact is that today, with pressure to produce student achievement scores that meet the requirements of state standards-based education reforms, as well as the Adequate Yearly Progress (AYP) accountability requirements of No Child Left Behind (NCLB), schools are increasingly finding themselves in a position of needing to change. Schools must make changes both to start the process of student achievement growth and to maintain that momentum over time. The changes schools make to achieve these goals are difficult and can take time to implement fully, but as you will see more of in the next chapter, they are remarkably similar across the country, in urban, suburban, and rural districts. This may be because, in this current policy environment as never before, schools everywhere are focused on educating *all* children to higher levels of achievement. Schools must therefore adapt their teaching strategies and develop their teachers in ways that were not universally expected before standards-based reform and NCLB.

The first section of this chapter discusses the pressures to improve student achievement that have led schools and districts to engage in the deep and fundamental change that is involved in program restructuring and resource reallocation. The second section of the chapter sets the macropractices we observed at various sites for creating and sustaining meaningful educational change into the large-scale, organizational change literature. We also note that Chapter 3 identifies the 10 steps that describe the actions schools and districts take to restructure, reallocate, and double student performance, thus providing many of the specifics of the change process.

1. PRESSURE FROM MULTIPLE SOURCES TO IMPROVE STUDENT ACHIEVEMENT

This section discusses the sources and nature of the pressures to improve dramatically student achievement in an effort to show that the catalyst for dramatic improvement can derive from multiple and many times reinforcing places, including pressure from the state, district, school, and federal levels. Each of these is addressed in turn, and where possible, examples of real districts and schools grappling with these pressures are given.

Pressure From State Standards-Based Reform

Even before NCLB was passed, many states had implemented some version of standards-based reform, many of them requiring a significant level of student progress to become proficient in the topics covered by the states' curriculum standards. At the district level, this tended to cause a flurry of activity to try to align what was being taught in the classroom with the state standards. (The logic being that students would do better on tests if they had actually been taught the curriculum covered by the test.)

Monroe, Wisconsin

In 2001, student scores on state standardized tests in the school district of Monroe were not satisfactory in the eyes of state and local administrators. In particular, the number of Monroe students whose scores were considered proficient on the 8th- and 10th-grade math tests was 37 percent and 46 percent, respectively, with state averages of 39 percent and 46 percent proficient. Since being at or below the state average was not where they wanted to be, the district had to make a number of changes to improve mathematics instruction. The hope also was that the changes would increase the number of students at or above the advanced level as well. The changes included a new math curriculum, content-focused professional development, and instructional coaches for teachers, and other changes that are discussed in more specificity in Chapters 1 and 5.

Milwaukee, Wisconsin

In Wisconsin's largest city, the test scores of the majority of its students were below the state average in terms of percentage of students at proficiency, and many students were scoring at the basic or below basic level. Given the threat of sanctions from NCLB and pressure from the state, Milwaukee's district leaders mounted a major plan for improving the schools. They established learning targets for every grade based on the state standards and distributed them to every classroom in every school (and all parents) in the district. The district also created the school-level position of implementer, whose job it was to ensure that the standards were being taught, which included making sure that teachers had the knowledge and skills they needed or creating professional development opportunities to help them acquire the necessary professional expertise. In addition, the district implemented a system of formative assessments so that students who were having trouble with the material concerning the standards were identified early and given help in the form of tutoring.

Pressure From District Administrators

Also feeling the heat from the federal and state level, district officials across the country have been working hard to meet the demands of the outcome-based framework in which they now find themselves operating. As a result, they are putting pressure on schools to make changes to their instructional delivery model (among other changes), which entails changing how resources are allocated.

Cordell Place in Washington

An example of this phenomenon occurred in a district outside Tacoma: A new superintendent came in and told schools they had to use their Title I money for research-based practices such as instructional coaches to help teachers develop their practice. This district's change process is profiled in the second section of this chapter.

District initiative to change is also the cases in Rosalia, Abbottsford, Monroe, Kennewick, and Madison.

Pressure From Within the School

At Farnham, an elementary school in the Midwest profiled in the first edition of this book, the desire for reform came from within the school. The principal, teachers, and parents were all dissatisfied with a part of the school's educational strategy. Teachers and parents believed class sizes were too large. The principal believed that the school's use of a traditional pullout program to serve students with special needs using categorical dollars such as Title I, English language learner (ELL), and special education were ineffective and stigmatizing to the students (mainly students of color) leaving the classroom for the services. For these reasons, the school arranged a series of retreats where all the stakeholders came together to redesign the school's educational strategy.

School-generated initiatives to dramatically improve were also the case for the Columbus School in Appleton, Franklin School in LaCrosse, and most of the schools profiled in Chenoweth (2007).

Pressure From the Federal Government

In this country, multiple layers of pressure to improve education are a part and parcel of the system. Constitutionally, education is viewed mainly as a task of the states, but the federal government has become increasingly involved over the last several decades. The federal role began in earnest when Title I, the federal compensatory education program, was passed in the 1960s. Although federal funding makes up a small portion (about 8 percent) of all spending for education, many schools depend on the money to finance programs that are critical to the success of low-income students. With the passage of the No Child Left Behind act in 2001, the federal government took on a much more active role in the education system, setting up multiple requirements for student progress on standardized tests and staffing classrooms with highly qualified teachers. These requirements placed a new level of pressure on states, districts, and schools.

In particular, NCLB's requirement that student test results be reported by subgroup (race, income, facility with the English language) meant that schools needed to ensure that the students in these subgroups, who were more likely to be low performing, were given the opportunity to reach proficiency. In many cases, this meant examining previous test results by subgroups, identifying what these students were not learning, and employing different instructional strategies so that these students could learn to the level of standards.

Columbus Elementary in Appleton, Wisconsin

This was exactly what happened at Columbus Elementary School in a small Wisconsin city. Over time, the number of non-English-speaking students attending the school increased, but the teaching strategies did not change, and, as a result, ELL students were underperforming on standardized tests and not meeting the AYP requirement of NCLB. Under the leadership of a new principal, the staff did an item-level analysis of previous test results and discovered what the ELL students were not learning or not able to communicate their knowledge about what they learned. As a result of this exploration, the staff decided to adopt a curriculum called Different Ways of Knowing, which was specifically designed to incorporate those with limited English proficiency into the regular classroom learning. In Chapter 1, you read more about how the new curriculum and the professional development provided to teachers enabled them to change classroom practice, resulting in higher test scores for all students at Columbus.

We should also note that the Reading First schools' success in Washington, as well as in many other states, were aided by this federal reading program, which was developed in the wake of the NCLB legislation.

2. THE LARGE-SCALE ORGANIZATIONAL CHANGE PROCESS

As the last section illustrated, the schools profiled in this book (and many others around the country) felt pressure from multiple sources and multiple directions, in many cases self-induced, to engage both in rethinking their overall educational strategies and making the related fiscal changes required to fully implement those strategies. In short, the schools became ready to engage in a large-scale, fundamental change process.

Section 2 has three subsections, which represent the three stages of the large-scale educational change process: (1) Laying the foundation for change, (2) Creating a new educational strategy, and (3) Implementing, monitoring, and continuous improvement.

Laying the Foundation for Change

As is true in other arenas, educational change is often spurred by recurring problems. Low academic achievement, lack of leadership at the school site, and teacher dissatisfaction are just a few of the problems that may prompt districts and schools to make major changes. But such changes need to be managed to make the overall restructuring and resource reallocation process successful. Researchers who have studied large-scale organizational change identify three key steps in this process (Mohrman & Cummings, 1989). Although they did not explicitly refer to the research on large-scale organizational change, nearly all the schools and districts studied for this book—those studied earlier when we focused more on resource reallocation and those studied more recently when we focused more on doubling student performance—nevertheless followed this three-part change process fairly closely.

The first step is called laying the foundation, which consists of the following:

Determining the values toward which the organization will be redesigned, acquiring learning and awareness about organizational design principles and alternatives, and diagnosing the current organization to gain awareness of the gap between the way the organization currently functions and how it needs to function to successfully achieve its values, given its environmental and technical requirements. (Mohrman, 1994, p. 206)

For schools and faculties undergoing such a change process, this step includes analyzing demographic and achievement data about the student population, reflecting on the values of the staff and school community regarding education and its purposes, and reaching a consensus as to the school's priorities for the future. This step can be referred to by a number of different names, including needs assessment and self-study.

Undergoing a needs assessment helps a school identify its strengths and weaknesses, thereby highlighting the areas that need to be the focus of change. But most important, analyzing data on all aspects of the school helps those professionals working in the school to understand the specifics of student performance by different content areas and different topics within each academic subject; how performance differs by race, income and gender; the specifics of student attendance and mobility; and what parents think about the school.

Such a data analysis exercise also produces two other elements that support school change. The first is school ownership of the data and the conclusions that are made; some might call this initial teacher "buy-in" to the need for change. The fact that the school faculty identifies and describes the strengths and weaknesses of the school themselves helps remove the tendency to deny the existence of problems and thus the need for change. Second, the process creates the thorough, detailed, and deep understanding of the school that allows the faculty to better match new educational strategies with the actual needs of the school.

For many schools or districts, this data analysis process can take up to a full year. Shortchanging this analytic step could prove detrimental to the success of the reforms that are chosen. The new strategies that schools choose must meet the particular needs of their school for faculties to be strongly committed to "buy into" them and to conclude that the change is worth the effort. To ensure that this happens, a deep and sound under-standing of a school's needs and a solid match with a new educational strategy are critical.

Nearly all of the schools and districts described in the first chapter went through this process of laying the foundation for large-scale change. Rosalia, Abbotsford, and Monroe all began with an analysis of state test data that pointed out shortcomings in their students' performance. Madison and Kennewick conducted more complex and comprehensive needs assessments. And the elementary schools in LaCrosse and Appleton also began with state assessment information that showed that large improvements in student achievement, especially for their lower-income and minority students, were badly needed.

One of the most comprehensive processes for laying the foundation for change took place in a district we studied earlier when we focused mainly on resource reallocation—Cordell Place. This district made a full year of self-study a prerequisite for gaining control of school funds and engaging in program restructuring and resource reallocation. Because this district's needs assessment was so thorough, we describe it in detail here as a model for other districts and schools to follow.

Cordell Place's new superintendent and other district leaders decided that their schools' low levels of student performance were unacceptable and needed to be raised. Since many of their schools qualified for signifi-cant amounts of federal Title I monies and could use those funds for schoolwide programs because their student poverty concentration exceeded 50 percent, the district decided to launch a major change process by offering these schools complete control over their Title I dollars. But the district set a condition. To gain discretion over Title I funds, schools had to agree to explore the possibilities for resource reallocation in an analytical manner by means of a self-study.

The self-study included an investigation by these schools' faculties of their student population, including attendance, mobility rates, and most importantly, student achievement. Various data were collected; both teachers and parents were surveyed. All of the information was analyzed by each school's faculty for the purpose of identifying the characteristics of the student population and then setting realistic though ambitious achievement goals. After the schools could describe the characteristics of their students with confidence, the district advised the schools to identify research-based strategies that would address their school's needs. If they could do so, they were then free to use Title I money to support that design or strategy.

Many of the school staff members who participated in the self-study attested to the value of the process, saying that it forced them to take a closer look at their students—demographic information as well as information regarding student mobility, attendance, and achievement—and learn who they were and what their academic strengths and weaknesses were. School staff members were able to dismiss anecdotes that other stakeholders used as suggestions for change in favor of data-driven conclusions derived from their own analysis of quantitative and qualitative student information. Through the process, they discovered they could make more informed decisions about what areas of the curriculum should be given special attention, as well as what social and community needs had to be addressed. Given this detailed picture of their schools, staff members felt well equipped to investigate curricular programs that had proved effective elsewhere and that fit their needs and their school philosophy.

Schools that engaged in resource reallocation in other districts engaged in similar data analysis processes. One elementary school's faculty began analyzing student performance data, the perceived and actual effectiveness of their strategies for helping students with special needs, and the satisfaction of both teachers and parents. They then organized two retreats to discuss this analysis with parents. They identified several different elements that were problematic with the school and assigned them to different parent/teacher committees. The proposal for improvement from all committees was to reduce class size, a strategy the school implemented the following year.

Another school became embroiled in a reconstitution process. After being identified as having consistently low levels of performance, the school was slated for reconstitution. A four-person district team consisting of two representatives from the teacher union and two administrative representatives orchestrated the reconstitution process. After assessing the characteristics of the student population, this team selected a new educational strategy for the school. In particular, it selected the Expeditionary Learning/Outward Bound design (www.elob.org) and augmented it with both a strong reading program (First Steps) and a strong mathematics program (TERC, available at www.terc.edu/). The team then selected a principal who was committed to the design. The principal, with the approval of the team, then selected lead teachers who also were committed to the new educational strategy. Last, the principal and lead teachers selected the remaining teaching staff, who all came aboard knowing exactly what educational strategy they were committing to and why. In this case, even though the school staff did not get to select the new strategy, the hiring process ensured that all staff members were invested in the new strategy.

In summation, the first step in laying the foundation for change is critical in establishing a shared understanding of the current condition of the school or district, the distance between actual performance and desired performance, and an understanding that accomplishing the new goals for much higher performance will entail large and complex organizational change. As Mohrman (1994) cautions, "Skipping this stage results in different participants enacting their different understandings and being at cross purposes . . . [and] failure to establish such an integrated understanding early in the change process leads to conflict and disillusionment" (p. 206).

We also saw this in our research. The change process in Rosalia was ignited and supported by administrative leaders who knew the research concerning what works, envisioned how to create change, sold the process, acted as change agents, and helped staff get past their resistance. However, during the first of five years, the district made the mistake of trying to skip the step of getting people on board and tried to implement change through administrative direction. They then realized that the staff needed to build ownership together and have more of a role in directing the process. A lot of their ultimate success was due to teachers' increased leadership role, professional development, and a common focus backed by hard work. As the administration took less of a lead, the teachers were given more and more autonomy and built up their own leadership skills so they were able to implement a decentralized teacher leadership model. The improvement process began with a centrally initiated vision, yet has been implemented from the bottom up.

Laying the foundation, in other words, is the first step in getting initial teacher "buy-in" to the change, restructuring, and resource reallocation processes. Full teacher buy-in or commitment to the overall effort emerges as the changes are implemented and teachers see that they work, that is, they produce gains in student performance. But this initial step is critically important both for making the next two steps substantive and for keeping teachers on board when implementation gets hard or unanticipated issues emerge.

Creating a New Educational Strategy

The second step in the change process requires analysis of the organizational and programmatic elements that can produce performance improvements in the desired areas. At this stage, participants in the change process choose the elements of the school that need changing to fix what needs to be fixed in the organization. Mohrman (1994) warns that laying the foundation (the first and previously described step) must be done in a comprehensive manner for this stage to be successful, or else the following may occur:

> Various change efforts in the organization will be designing changes that do not complement one another. The organization will have to recycle into a stage of clarifying values and identifying criteria. The design piece of large-scale change is much easier if there are agreement and understanding of the criteria for successful change. (p. 208)

In other words, participants in the change process must spend time reaching a consensus for a unified vision of the future of the organization. Then, having assessed the needs of the school and researched strategies for improvement, the next step is to choose the full complement of educational strategies that best meet the needs of their school.

Creating a new educational strategy requires consciously making decisions about the regular education program as well as about programs and services for struggling students that need extra help to achieve to proficiency. There are many decisions that must be made about the regular education program. The first is the overall education program, particularly the curriculum and instructional strategies. Some schools select one of several existing national, comprehensive school designs, such as the Different Ways of Knowing for Columbus Elementary. Others adapted pieces from different designs. Still others adopted a more rigorous curriculum, program by program. And a few schools were successful in creating their own standards-based curriculum programs, like the Madison reading program.

Each school's educational strategy also required conscious attention to several related issues that largely drive a school's cost. For example, a school that identifies low reading scores as the most glaring need will want to consider the most effective reading program, the ideal reading class sizes, the best ways to group students for reading, and the professional development teachers will need to successfully teach the new reading program. Many of the schools and districts profiled in Chapter 1, as well as those studied earlier in our reallocation analysis, identified low reading scores as the number one problem that needed to be addressed, but they took a variety of approaches to restructuring their reading programs. Some adopted a comprehensive external program, such as Success for All (www.successforall.net). Others adopted the Open Court book series. Other schools implemented small class sizes of 15 and also adopted a new, more phonics-based reading curriculum. All of these decisions had cost implications. As was clear for all the cases in Chapter 1, all new curriculum decisions were then followed by extensive professional development. Success for All requires tutors and schoolwide instructional facilitators, small class sizes usually require more teachers, and all curricular changes require extensive professional development for teachers to be successful. Schools made these decisions consciously and were aware that they would need to reallocate resources to implement them, as well as find new grants in some cases.

As fully part of their new educational strategies, the schools also made dramatic new choices about serving struggling students that needed extra help to learn to good performance levels. Of course, all had some percentage of struggling students or students who needed extra help to learn to the level of the performance standards. Moreover, the new strategies most schools implemented did not make fine distinctions between a low-achieving student, a struggling student from a low-income background, a student who had to learn English as well as academic content, or a student with some type of mild learning disability. The schools viewed all these students as "struggling" to meet the new and higher performance standards, and therefore, they used their new educational strategies to help all of these students. Furthermore, as described later in this book, some schools pooled the funds that accompanied these different student labels to afford the more powerful strategies of their new educational program.

Although the amount and specific type of additional help needed by each student varied widely, most schools dramatically reduced or eliminated the pullout resource room strategies with which they were dissatisfied. (Those students with severe disabilities continued to be served in self-contained classrooms, thus were not affected by the school restructuring or resource reallocation process.) They then implemented some combination of one-to-one tutoring, instruction in small classes of about 15, before- and afterschool academic tutoring, and summer school. Although each particular strategy for struggling students had the goal of educating those students to the same high performance standards as all other students, they also required resources that were found both by resource reallocation and new grants.

Several schools moved pullout teachers, who had dual licensure in both regular and special education, into regular classrooms and mainstreamed all but the severely disabled students. This practice also enabled schools to reduce class size by increasing the number of classroom teachers. And by adopting a dual licensure strategy for its teachers, the schools ensured that the expertise needed for each class of students was in place. Other schools and districts had all teachers provide reading instruction and put the most expert teachers with the students who had the most challenging problems.

Schools also made decisions about how to use teachers' time. Several schools rescheduled the teaching day to provide 60 to 90 minutes of planning time at least four to five times each week. Other schools altered the schedule so that all teachers on the same teaching team had their preparation period at the same time to enable them to meet as a team. Some schools added time to four days and then dismissed students early on the fifth day, thus giving teachers two to three hours of uninterrupted planning time. Nearly all schools created and implemented new strategies for giving teachers more uninterrupted, and often collaborative, planning time during the regular school day to provide the time for preparation and professional development needed to implement their new educational strategy.

Many other strategies that serve this purpose can be funded via resource reallocation; the important thing is for schools to identify strategies that meet the needs of their students and then staff and structure the school accordingly. These changes often are accompanied by a series of new policies as well, ranging from requirements for teacher licensure to enhanced training.

By structuring, scheduling, and staffing the schools according to the imperatives of their new educational strategy, the schools began allocating resources to where they were needed most and could have the largest impact on achievement. Without a new educational strategy—or vision—schools would not have known what resources to drop and what resources to add. Chapters 4, 5, and 6 provide the details of multiple strategies for how schools lowered class sizes, expanded professional development days, put instructional coaches into schools, and provided tutoring, extended-day homework help, and summer school—all effective but resource-intensive strategies.

Implementation, Monitoring, and Continuous Improvement

The third step in a large-scale, organizational change process, which certainly describes both school restructuring and resource reallocation, is implementation, monitoring, and continuous improvement. As schools start implementing their new educational strategies, they must attempt to monitor both the extent of their implementation and the early effects on student performance and seek to maintain and improve their strategies.

It should be clear that this third step is not the same as simply implementing a new educational strategy. To be sure, the schools and districts studied all began implementing their new educational strategy. And they exerted efforts to ensure that they were fully implementing all elements of their new educational strategy, in part because they knew from reviewing research that full implementation was required to produce the desired effects (Cooper, Slavin, & Madden, 1997; Haynes, Emmons, & Woodruff, 1998; Huberman & Miles, 1984; Stringfield & Datnow, 1998).

But even though all the schools had put together a new educational strategy that they believed would help them improve their students' performance, the level of performance improvement they needed to produce was often greater than the strategy they had selected had produced in other schools. Thus, the schools believed that their new educational strategy would begin to improve student performance, but they also knew they would need to do even more—that full implementation of their new strategy was necessary but not sufficient to achieve the goals they were trying to attain.

For example, several schools studied during our research on resource reallocation began the restructuring and resource redeployment process by implementing the Success for All reading program. This required a complete change in their reading program; new forms of student grouping, including cross-grade ability grouping for reading; more professional development; a full-time instructional facilitator; and tutors. Initial implementation required substantial program restructuring and different use of school dollars.

But in the second year, some schools decided to strengthen the program, for example, by adding an additional teacher-tutor. Other schools that had been using the reading program for one to two years decided to adopt the program's mathematics program as well. Many of these same schools were planning to add the integrated science–social studies World-Lab program in the fourth and fifth year. In short, though the schools began with a fairly bold restructuring plan for reading, they extended and improved it over time by changing other core-curricular areas as well. This also was true for many of the districts and schools doubling performance; most began with a reading focus but soon expanded to math and some even to science.

Many of the schools and districts that sought to double performance moved through a similar transformation and reformulation implementation process. District initiatives started in voluntary schools, and each year more schools joined the initiative. In other districts, training initially focused on trainers of trainers, so over time the districts could provide the training for all teachers.

The schools that had adopted a class-size reduction program also began analyzing their reading and mathematics curriculum programs more seriously. Although they had "bet" pretty much their entire school budget on the small class-size strategy, they soon realized that small classes alone might not be a powerful enough change. Some concluded that small class sizes together with a stronger reading program, in which all teachers would be trained, would likely be even more effective than small classes alone.

We also heard hints from some teachers that spending the bulk of the school budget on small class sizes might not have been the best strategy. They wondered whether classes in the range of 20—that is, smaller than 25 to 30 but larger than 15—together with some teacher-tutors for struggling students might be a stronger strategy than very small classes for all subjects every day without any additional support for struggling students.

Because the schools studied tended to be in their second or third year of implementation, we cannot say for sure what might happen in subsequent years. But we can raise the above cautions and make the following suggestions. Each school needs to monitor the results of their efforts on student performance each and every year. They need to know whether the new strategies they are implementing are having the desired effects, where the strategies are not having the desired effects, and to be aware of other issues and challenges as they arise.

School restructuring to produce the goals of current standards-based education reform is not a one-year or even a discrete two- or three-year effort. It might take a decade or longer to fully accomplish all goals. Therefore, schools need to view themselves as engaging in an ongoing restructuring, analysis, monitoring, reframing, and improvement process, that is, a continuous change process.

To be sure, it is imperative that schools start with a good understanding of their current situation and a strong belief that the new educational strategies they select will dramatically improve their students' learning. But not all programs will be as effective as desired. Further, conditions and demands can change, and midcourse corrections may be required. Thus, the third part of the change process is recognizing that the kinds of change and improvement in performance required by current standards-based reform will require schools to engage in a continuous change and improvement process over numerous years.

SUMMARY

In today's policy environment, schools and districts are feeling the pressure to help all students succeed. As a result, many are undergoing program restructuring and resource reallocation, which together constitute a large-scale change effort. Schools contemplating tackling this agenda would be smart to understand this fact and design and manage a careful change process. Significant time should be spent laying the foundation for the change by engaging all key actors in analyzing school-specific data. This gives school faculties a comprehensive and detailed understanding of conditions at the school, particularly the nature and level of student performance. Next, faculties should spend time creating a new educational strategy on the basis of the conclusions from the data analysis. Finally, schools should understand that the full implementation of the new educational strategy is required in the short term, but that over time, the new strategy might need to be augmented and changed to produce the higher levels of performance required.

All three steps of this complex change process are critical. Throughout this book, you will note references to the steps that schools must take to help ensure the success of their chosen reforms. Moreover, when you read about the schools profiled in the last chapter, you probably noted that to varying degrees, all of them underwent a change process on their way to doubling student performance. Chapter 3 then distills this information into 10 steps schools and districts go through as they "double performance." These 10 steps fit within this more macro-change process described above but provide more detailed and nuanced information of exactly what schools and districts did to dramatically improve student learning.

Ten Steps to Double Student Performance

As we developed the short cases in Chapter 1 of schools and districts doubling performance, we and many of our colleagues began to realize the striking similarities of the processes across the cases. These hunches were confirmed by reading other case studies of dramatically improving schools and districts (Chenoweth, 2007; Childress, Elmore, Grossman, & Johnson, 2007; Supovitz, 2006). Although the change literature in education stresses the importance of context, the interpretation of that emphasis often has been that dramatically improving schools across the country will require very different processes in different kinds of districts and schools, even different for every district and school. That is not what we have found. As this chapter shows, the general processes are quite similar—regardless of the size of the school or district, location in a rural, suburban, or urban environment, or student demographic characteristics.

To be sure, context was addressed by all cases, as the carefully construed bottom-up strategy in Madison (described in Chapter 1) reflects. And there were differences in many specifics across the schools and districts; they did not all adopt the same reading or mathematics program, nor did they all organize the instructional program in the same way, nor face the same political or institutional constraints.

However, despite differences in specifics, there were strong similarities in the core elements that constituted the changes these schools and districts implemented as they doubled student performance. We have distilled these elements into 10 steps in the process of doubling performance. There is no magic to our finding 10 steps. Some analysts might combine one or two of our steps into a larger step. Furthermore, our 10 steps are quite similar to the six principles for avoiding failure and improving performance discussed by Blankstein (2004) and quite similar to the six lessons for high performance that Kati Haycock, president of the Education Trust, concludes from that organization's multiple studies of schools that are successful in producing high levels of academic achievement in schools characterized by high-poverty and high-minority student populations (see, e.g., her concluding presentation at the 2007 Wisconsin Doubling Performance Conference at http://www.education.wisc.edu/elpa/conferences/WILA/2007%20 Presentations/PPPresentations/KatiHaycockKeynote.ppt).

Finally, our 10 steps are quite compatible with the strategies in the collection of cases of urban school reform in Childress et al. (2007) and very aligned with their suggestions for how to manage urban districts (Childress, Elmore, and Grossman, 2006).

Moreover, the 10 steps discussed in this chapter "unpack" the more macro three steps of the large-scale organizational change process discussed at the end of Chapter 2. Thus, this chapter is consistent with the large-scale organizational change literature but provides more detail that is specific to educational organizations—schools and districts—as they move forward and are successful in dramatically improving student performance. We present the 10 steps in what appears as a chronological order, which was the case for some schools, but the order of the steps is not crucial; other schools and districts might move through the steps in a different order, sometimes even cycling back to some previous step and moving forward from that point again.

STEP 1: UNDERSTANDING THE PERFORMANCE PROBLEM AND CHALLENGE

The first step is pretty much the same as the first step of the change process discussed in Chapter 2, namely, engaging in a variety of activities to understand the performance status/problems of the school or district and to fully understand the distance between current and desired performance.

To gain an understanding of the current performance situation, all the schools and districts began by analyzing state testing data. The state testing data not only gave specific information on the overall status of student achievement but also gave information on achievement in different subtopics of each content area tested. For example, Monroe discovered that while its students did well on basic skills in mathematics, they did not do well on the problem-solving tasks. Other districts discovered that while the overall level of performance was fine, the district average was a combination of much higher performance for the white students and much lower performance for their low-income and minority students, a situation that was not defendable. Madison, Wisconsin, found that if students were below the basic level in the third grade, those students never achieved beyond the basic level by the eighth grade and that the bulk of students in this category were African Americans. A school from our reallocation studies found that test scores not only differed by student demographic characteristics but also that the pullout services during the school day "segregated" students by color and devised a strategy to undo both the performance segmentation as well as the service segregation.

So nearly all schools and districts began their trek toward doubling performance by analyzing their students' test scores from the state testing program. We should add that none of the places studied spent much time criticizing the state tests or arguing that the tests assessed too narrow a version of achievement. The individuals may have had criticisms, and those criticisms may have been valid, but they all used the state tests as a starting point for understanding where they stood vis-à-vis student performance and used the results of the analysis to identify the macro areas where they needed to improve.

We also should note that the places we studied did not focus this analytic phase on student, family, or community demographics in large part because they were not actionable on the part of schools.[1] They analyzed student performance data on the assumption that what schools did largely impacted student academic performance and that to improve performance, a sophisticated understanding of the extant performance condition of the school and district was an essential first step.

Many of the schools and districts also engaged in a curriculum-mapping process during this beginning stage, comparing what content was taught in various subjects, particularly reading and mathematics, and what content was assessed on the state tests. In many cases, they discovered that they were not teaching some of the content on the test. As mentioned in Chapter 1, this was exactly the situation in Rosalia with writing. Writing scores on the state test were low, and when the response was to begin teaching more writing, student scores on the state test rose dramatically, which proved that students will do better on tests when they are taught what the tests measure.

Another aspect of the curriculum mapping was aligning the state tests, with the state and district curriculum content standards, with what teachers actually taught and then modifying the school and district curriculum to align more closely with the state curriculum standards and the scope of the state testing program.

Put differently, all schools and districts on the road to doubling student performance began by analyzing their student performance data. They did not begin by saying they needed more money, they did not begin by criticizing the obvious flaws of the No Child Left Behind (NCLB) program, and they did not begin by analyzing student demographics. They began analyzing data that measured the performance of their students. The goal was to understand the performance situation for their district and school, to see where students were performing well and where they were not, to understand differences in performance by student subgroups, and to understand how far or close their students' performance was to proficient and advanced levels of performance as indicated by state tests.

STEP 2: SET AMBITIOUS GOALS

The second step is to set very high and ambitious goals regardless of the current performance level or student demographics. The Madison and Kennewick districts set a goal of having 90 percent or more of students by the end of Grade 3 with proficient scores on the reading test. The Stanton Elementary school in Philadelphia (Chenoweth, 2007), an all-minority and nearly all-poverty school, set a goal of having the bulk of students achieve to the advanced level of performance. As its principal Barbara Adderly said, "If you focus on advanced levels of performance, proficiency will take care of itself." As described in Chapter 1, this also worked for the Monroe district; by addressing performance shortcomings in areas that constituted advanced performance levels, they not only boosted performance at the proficiency levels but also more than doubled performance at the advanced levels.

When the principal that began the process of improvement in Elmont Junior/Senior High School (Chenoweth, 2007) first entered the school, the departing administrator said, "Welcome to one of the best, minority high schools in the state of New York." The new principal decided to change that perception by asking, "Why just a good minority high school? Let's make this one of the best, overall high schools in the state." And with his school team, he set a goal of having all students pass all the New York State Regents tests, which are among the most rigorous end-of-course examinations in the country. The goal of the recently opened Baltimore Talent Development High School, which presented at the 2007 Wisconsin Doubling Performance Conference, is to have all students graduate and be eligible to attend college, an atypical and ambitious goal for an all-minority, high-poverty school in the middle of Baltimore City.

Similarly, as described in Chapter 1, Rosalia, in rural northwestern Washington, set a goal for all of their students to achieve to proficiency in reading and mathematics and to be able to think analytically. Abbotsford, Wisconsin, set a goal of having 90 percent of all students achieve at least to the proficiency level and nearly attained this goal even though the percentages of low-income, immigrant, and ELL students rose every year. The Victory School in Milwaukee labeled all their students gifted and talented even though the bulk of their students were from lower-income and minority backgrounds; the school ignored demographics and set high expectations, and as the teachers and students responded, student test scores rose.

The point here is threefold. First, all the districts and schools that have doubled performance set very high goals; they strived for "quantum improvements" in performance not just marginal improvements. To many educators, these goals might seem unattainable, but they are set very high nevertheless, and the schools believed they could be attained. Second, the goals apply to all students, including low-income and minority students; schools and districts doubling performance seek to break the confinements of student demographics; they do not want to be seen as the best poverty school or the best minority school, that is, just beating the odds, but be seen as a top school period, regardless of the demographic composition of their student body. Third, even if the schools and districts did not attain their ambitious goals, they would make huge progress toward their goals, and thus, be in a much better place than where they started. So if the goal is to have 90 percent of all low-income and minority students achieve to or above proficiency, from a position of say 30 percent today, having 85 percent at that level after a five-year period of hard work would not be considered a failure. Although the specific goal of 90 percent might not have been reached, boosting proficiency performance from the 30 percent level to the 85 percent level represents a huge and significant improvement.

It should be clear that the people in these schools and districts believed that all children could learn to high levels, including children from poverty, minority, and non-English-speaking backgrounds. They were not befuddled by the demographics or characteristics of their students. They simply saw their job as educating students to high standards and set high goals for student performance regardless of the sociodemographic conditions of their students, school, or community. Furthermore, doubling performance can be done by large urban districts as well. Indeed, Boston tripled the performance of its students on the state math test over a five- to eight-year period; Montgomery County Public Schools in Maryland, that now has growing percentages of low-income and minority students, has 90 percent of its very youngest children performing at or above state standards, including all key student subgroups; and districts such as Aldine (Texas), Long Beach (California), and New York City have given large boosts to student academic performance—so it is possible to set and meet high goals for nearly all districts.

Finally, none of the schools and districts studied had a goal just of getting the "bubble" kids over the proficiency bar. Although the practice of focusing on the kids just below the proficiency standard has appeared in some research across the country, that practice in part reflects a very modest goal and does not lead to large, long-term, student performance gains. It might produce one year of adequate yearly progress, but it would be inconsistent with districts trying to double student performance or educating 90 percent to 95 percent of students to a proficient or advanced level.

In short, after understanding the complexities of the current status of student performance in their school or districts, the places that doubled performance set very high goals for the future—getting all students up to or beyond a proficiency bar, focusing on educating a large portion of students to the advanced level of performance, or having all students pass end-of-course examinations or graduate from high school. In a very real sense, these goals are more than just "stretch" goals; they are ambitious goals that, in most cases, neutral observers would say could not be met. But as the cases we and others (e.g., Chenoweth, 2007) profiled show, the goals were met by these districts and schools.

STEP 3: CHANGE THE CURRICULUM PROGRAM AND CREATE A NEW INSTRUCTIONAL VISION

Step 3 addresses the core educational issues that are the prime issues that educators in schools can change: the curriculum and instructional program. Schools that produce high levels of student performance focus on what they can impact—everything that happens in schools: the assignment of teachers, the organization of curriculum and instruction, academic expectations, and curriculum and instruction. They do not focus on poverty, the lack of health care for many urban children, problems with parent involvement, full funding of NCLB, the problems with the state testing system, or the accountability glitches of NCLB. They address the pieces of the education system over which they have control. And that allows them to act.

This was true for all the schools and districts we studied. Using the language of the large-scale educational change process, Step 3 entailed framing a new educational vision for the school, which for most schools included a complete redesign of the district and/or school curriculum and instructional program.

To put the case bluntly, the schools threw out their old curriculum programs and books and either created or bought new programs. Kennewick adopted the Open Court reading program, Monroe adopted the Everyday Math program, which several other elementary schools in other cases also adopted. Abbotsford switched to a guided reading program, and Madison created its own "balanced" reading program that stressed a balance of reading comprehension, writing, and phonics. Franklin Elementary in LaCrosse adopted Math Investigations.

Because of its increasing number of ELL students and goal to have all students learn to high standards and to restructure the entire school, Columbus Elementary in Appleton, Wisconsin, selected the schoolwide Different Ways of Knowing program. Several schools profiled in the first edition of this book, when we focused on resource reallocation, selected comprehensive school designs, including Success for All, the Modern Red Schoolhouse, Expedition Learning/Outward Bound, and Core Knowledge. The concept behind both of these types of changes is similar: to choose what in the view of the local educators is a new, research-based strategy for the school that fits the particular needs of its students.

Because Elmont Junior/Senior High School wanted all students to take and pass Regents tests, the school threw out all former remedial and general education courses and included only courses aligned with the New York Regents exams. Baltimore Talent Development High School restructured the entire ninth-grade program to have a more personalized organization that focused on the transition to high school, gave all students rigorous academic programs, and then allowed students to specialize in certain areas for Grades 10–12.

We have found no case of a school or district that simply worked harder at the curriculum and instructional program that existed when they engaged in the Step 1 analysis of their students' state test data. Consciously or unconsciously, they all decided that the old curriculum program had gotten them to their existing performance level, which was not good enough, and that something different, more powerful, and more rigorous was needed to help them attain their new ambitious goals.

One clear theme for Step 3 is adopting a new curriculum program in all content areas but particularly reading and mathematics. We are not in a position to assess the correctness or rigor of all the programs selected. We cannot say that all of the programs were "research-based," though many of the individuals in the schools made that claim. We would refer readers to the Best Evidence Encyclopedia (BEE: www.bestevidence.org), which provides research-based reviews of reading and math programs for elementary, middle, and high schools, reading programs for ELL students, and many comprehensive school reform designs. This and other Web sites, such as the What Works Clearinghouse (http://ies.ed.gov/ncee/wwc), provide advice on what programs research has proven to be effective.

In addition to new curriculum programs, Step 3 also includes, over time, the development of a schoolwide and often districtwide view of what good instructional practice is and looks like in classrooms. This was especially true for reading and mathematics. Districts such as Kennewick and Madison not only created a systemic approach to the reading curriculum that was to be implemented in all schools but also a systemic approach to reading instructional practice. Teachers worked at developing this view of instruction collaboratively—through professional learning communities—as a way to implement the new reading program. This new way of teaching reading permeated new teacher induction, ongoing professional development for experienced teachers, and often made it into the district's evaluation system as well. In the process, instructional practice became "public" in that teachers talked together about good instructional practice, worked at it in their own classrooms, had it demonstrated for them by instructional coaches, and made it a goal that over time all teachers would deploy instruction according to this new vision.

This creation of a shared sense of good instructional practice, together with new curriculum programs, is how teachers made a big difference in student learning. When educators cite the research that teachers have the largest impact on student achievement, what is underneath the claim is teachers' instructional practice—both what they teach and how they teach it. The best teachers deploy different instructional practices than other teachers; that is why they are more effective. The widely known case of District 2 in New York City (Elmore & Burney, 1999) had this as a central core of the district's efforts; all efforts were orchestrated around a new view of how to teach reading. And the schools and districts we studied that doubled performance developed new understandings of effective teaching as well as a culture that required all teachers to learn these instructional practices and use them with their students. Indeed, part of the Madison story is that teachers demanded more and more specifics about the balanced approach to reading instruction that all teachers were expected to implement, and as those views of reading instructional practice took hold in the primary grades, both upper elementary and middle school teachers asked for the same development focus for those grade levels as well.

In short, during Step 3, schools threw out their old curriculum programs and books, replaced them with new curriculum programs, and simultaneously over time collaboratively developed more effective ways to teach that curriculum that all teachers were supposed to learn and implement in their classrooms. They changed the curriculum and instructional program and made it systemic across all schools in the district.

Going somewhat beyond the data in our cases, we suggest that all schools and districts review the vision of accomplished teaching that is embodied in the 24 standards of the National Board for Professional Teaching Standards (NBPTS). These documents represent a consensus of what many of the top teachers, political, education, and business leaders in the country consider high quality instruction. Districts could use these standards to "drive" quality instructional practice throughout all schools and classrooms, including developing and placing in lead positions National Board Certified Teachers—that is, individuals who have shown that their instructional practice meets the high and rigorous standards for board certification. Although some have interpreted the research as somewhat mixed, the most statistically sophisticated studies show that National Board Certified Teachers are effective teachers and produce some of the largest student-learning gains; Goldhaber, Perry, and Anthony (2004) and Goldhaber and Anthony (2005) show that those who seek National Board Certification are among the best teachers and that among that group of good teachers, those who become certified produce more learning gains than those who do not get certified.

STEP 4: FORMATIVE ASSESSMENTS AND DATA-BASED DECISION MAKING

It may surprise some readers to learn that Step 4 includes implementing more testing, even beyond what is required by the state or NCLB. Contrary to the widespread complaints in many education circles that there is too much testing in America's schools, the places we studied that doubled performance actually added another layer of testing—formative assessments. Formative assessments are instruments designed to provide detailed and concrete information on what students know and do not know with respect to discrete curriculum units. When teachers have this information, they are able to design instructional activities that are more precisely tailored to the exact learning status of the students in their own classrooms and school. In this way, their instruction can be, to use a term from the business community, much more efficient: They know the goals and objectives they want students to learn, they know exactly what their students do and do not know with respect to those goals and objectives, so they craft instructional activities specifically to help the students in their classrooms learn the goals and objectives for the particular curriculum unit.

Formative assessments are a new but rapidly evolving educational tool (see Boudett & Steele, 2007; Boudett, City, & Murnane, 2007). Plus, there are many sources and types of formative assessments. One type, used by many of the schools and districts we studied, is available from the Northwest Evaluation Association (NWEA) (www.nwea.org) in Portland, Oregon. Because the NWEA and MAP (Measures of Academic Progress) assessments are online, teachers receive the results the next day so they can immediately use them in their weekly instructional planning. Since the NWEA and MAP tests are administered quarterly, some educators refer to them as "benchmark" assessments, and reserve the term "formative" assessments for instruments that can be used for shorter segments of instruction. Many of the schools and districts we studied, however, used the NWEA assessments and referred to them as formative assessments. The core point is that they had tests that were administered more often than the annual state accountability tests.

Many Reading First schools use the Dynamic Indicators of Basic Early Literacy Skills (DIBELS) formative assessments (http://dibels.uoregon.edu). Madison, Wisconsin, taught all teachers to take the "running records" that generally are part of the Reading Recovery tutoring program and use them as the basis for the formative assessment analysis in that district. Kennewick, Washington, uses a similar tool called MAP, designed by the NWEA to help schools learn more about their students' understanding of reading, mathematics, and language usage and use that information to guide their teaching. The Wireless Generation (www.wirelessgeneration.com) has created a formative assessment that can be used with a handheld electronic device. The company also offers a Web service that provides information on how to turn the results into specific, instructional strategies; the Web service also provides professional development for teachers including video clips of how to teach certain reading skills. Musti-Rao and Cartledge (2007) identified a number of additional reading assessment batteries, and Jordan (2007) identified a screening instrument that assesses number-sense knowledge of elementary children, which is a basic concept for understanding arithmetic.

Most of the formative and benchmark assessments, many of which are now online, can be accessed for a fee of between $25 and $35 per student, which would cover assessments for four subjects and the handheld devices in some cases. The school finance adequacy model discussed in Chapter 7 includes $25 per pupil for such assessments.

Most teachers and principals in the elementary and middle schools we studied said that while analysis of the state tests provided a good beginning for them to redesign their educational program, they needed the additional, more microlevel, formative (or benchmark) assessment and other screening data to design the details of and daily lesson plans for curriculum units that were more effective in getting all students to learn the main objectives of the unit to proficiency.

It is an irony in this age of complaints about too much testing that the schools and districts doubling performance actually expanded testing! To be sure, these effective educational organizations agreed that mere testing did not make students learn more, but they stated very strongly that while state tests provided them with a macromap of where the school had been effective and where it had been ineffective, the formative assessments were needed to provide a micromap for how they needed to teach specific curriculum units and to boost performance that the macrotests measured.

However, although analysis of the macro-issues were relatively straightforward once faculties in schools were given access to test data, particularly the items in the state tests, analysis of the microdata from the formative assessments was much more difficult. Analyses of state tests indicated topics that were not taught in the curriculum, such as writing, or expectations that were not met, such as problem solving in mathematics. These were quite straightforward to remedy—teach more writing and embed more authentic problem solving in the math curriculum.

But the formative assessments were more difficult to translate into instructional practices. When a teacher had the "running record" for his or her 25 elementary students, it was not easy to design instructional strategies that addressed the learning profile of each student. That took an expertise that most teachers did not have, and that in part led to Step 5— intensive, ongoing professional development. See Boudett et al. (2007) and the Wireless Generation (www.wirelessgeneration.com) for examples of how to interpret formative assessment data and translate them into concrete and student-specific, appropriate instructional strategies. The entire issue of *Educational Leadership* (December 2007/January 2008) also has many interesting examples of how formative assessments can be used in the instructional improvement process.

A Comment on Resources

It should be clear that the first four steps require very modest resources. As noted, purchasing access to formative assessments costs approximately $25 to $35 per student, hardly a big dent in any district budget, and again, a resource included in the school finance adequacy model discussed in Chapter 7. Although analyzing state test scores, setting high goals and expectations, and reviewing and then adopting new curriculum and instruction programs take some time, the activities themselves require at most a small amount of money. Buying new textbooks and instructional materials takes money, but all districts already have funds for such expenditures, so in the medium term, those expenditures can be absorbed into ongoing regular budgets. The next set of steps, however, requires a more significant level of resources to implement.

STEP 5: ONGOING, INTENSIVE PROFESSIONAL DEVELOPMENT

Step 5 is the deployment of widespread, systemic, and ongoing professional development. This was a uniform finding from all schools and districts, and it makes good sense. Often, the initial analysis of state testing data entails some professional development as not all teachers and principals are skilled in analyzing the meaning of state test data. Furthermore, the adoption of new curriculum programs requires additional professional development to help all teachers acquire the expertise to teach the new curricular materials well; moreover, most of the professional development linked to the new textbooks and other curriculum materials was provided by district staff or other consultants and not by the textbook companies. In addition, extensive and ongoing professional development is needed as the schools and districts work to develop the system's new approach to good instruction; such professional development around new instructional practices continues for several years and has not stopped in any of the places we studied that doubled performance. Finally, considerable professional development is needed on how to take the information from the formative assessments and design instructional programs that meet the needs of the students in each classroom.

Good, ongoing professional development requires resources. In fact, there are three primary resources needed to mount the type of professional development programs we found in the schools and districts studied. The first is pupil-free teacher days during which time teachers receive training. Pupil-free days can be accomplished in two ways. One way is by hiring substitute teachers and providing professional development during the regular school year; this strategy, though, reduces time for teachers to instruct students and was therefore the least-followed strategy in the schools and districts we studied. The other way to provide pupil-free days is by extending the school year for teachers and providing professional development during the summer usually before the school year starts or during days spaced throughout the year when students are not present. To provide the appropriate remuneration, either teachers are paid daily stipends for these days, or the teacher contract year is extended. The cost for either is about the same. The schools and districts we studied provided approximately 10 days of pupil-free time for teacher professional development. This resource is included in the school finance adequacy model discussed in Chapter 7.

A second cost is funds for trainers. Whether the trainers are external consultants, technical assistance providers part of comprehensive school designs, or central office, professional development staff, funds are needed to cover the training costs. In a few cases, districts were able to access support staff from regional education offices, but most often, even these individuals charged fees for services provided, especially if they were long-term services. The school finance adequacy model discussed in Chapter 7 includes $100 per pupil to cover the cost of trainers.

A third cost is for instructional facilitators or instructional coaches. These individuals who work in schools, often on a full-time basis, and provide the in-classroom coaching assistance that is key to making professional development work lead to change in instructional practice that produces student learning gains (for a review of the key features of effective professional development and their costs, see Odden, Archibald, Fermanich, & Gallagher, 2002). The creation of instructional coach, lead teacher, mentor, and head teacher positions, all labels for essentially the same role, distinguishes the professional development initiatives from most of those in the past and appears to be a "secular" trend around the country. Again, this resource is included in the school finance adequacy model discussed in Chapter 7.

We discuss more in Chapter 5 about how schools and districts reallocated resources to fund some of these professional development costs but wanted simply to describe here the elements that were needed to deploy the kinds of intensive and ongoing professional development that we found in the schools and districts studied. As indicated, all these professional development resources are included in the school finance adequacy model in Chapter 7.

Another requirement for professional development is some time during the regular school day for collaboration among teaches and the instructional coaches on the instructional program. This time is usually available if the school has staff for elective classes such as art, music, and physical education because when students are in elective classes, their regular content teachers are not teaching and have time to collaborate on curriculum and instruction. If elective teachers are not provided, then schools usually extend the teacher work day to provide time for teacher collaborative work. The adequacy model in Chapter 7 includes resources for specialist and elective teachers, so it provides this time for collaborative work by teachers.

In many cases, some of the most collaborative professional development occurs when groups of teachers meet, usually with the instructional coaches, to discuss the results of the formative assessments and create new teaching strategies and instructional units specifically tailored to the needs of the students as revealed in the formative assessment data. This is complex work. Often, the instructional coach is able to identify professional development topics for teachers based on the struggles teachers might have in moving from the assessment data to finely honed instructional units. So the products of these sessions are both professional development for teachers and more finely targeted curriculum units and instructional strategies for students. These are the kinds of ongoing teacher collaborative work that produced "professional learning communities" in nearly all of the schools and districts studied.

Professional development resources also are needed to provide the new and experienced teacher mentoring that can be extraordinarily helpful in guiding new teachers successfully into the teaching profession and experienced teachers into broadening their instructional expertise. Shulman and Sato (2006) provide guidance for how to structure effective mentoring programs.

As the Madison and Monroe cases indicated, however, districts are not always able fiscally to maintain this level of intensive professional development, even though research shows that this is how to make professional development work see Odden et al. (2002). Madison rotated reading coaches among its highest poverty schools, and Monroe felt it was able to afford math coaches for only one year. The reading coaches were multiyear staff in the Washington Reading First schools but supported largely by the federal Reading First grant.

Whether or not resources are available to support needed funding long term, and Chapter 7 makes it clear that an "adequate" school funding system would provide these resources, this step makes it clear that extensive, comprehensive professional development, with instructional coaches and focused explicitly on the reading and mathematics program—or other targeted content areas—was a core part of the multiple strategies deployed by all schools and districts that doubled performance.

STEP 6: USING TIME EFFICIENTLY AND EFFECTIVELY

Step 6 concerns the use of what is generally considered a fixed resource: instructional time during the regular school day. And to use business terms, these schools and districts used time more efficiently and more effectively.

There are several examples of better use of time. Most elementary schools set aside a large amount of time for reading, generally 90 minutes but in some cases (Kennewick, for one), 120 minutes per day. Furthermore, during reading and at least also mathematics instruction, interruptions were not allowed; all the minutes devoted to reading and math were "protected" from outside factors so teachers could use all of that time to provide instruction in these critical subject areas.

Other schools organized students into cross-age groups based on their reading achievement levels; in this way, teachers could use the entire 90 minutes for whole group instruction as the students were essentially at the same level in reading. Schools that did not use such student grouping generally had to divide the students into two to three groups, each of which received less instructional time than the students in the classes all on the same level.

One of the schools we studied in Kennewick used a combination of both of these strategies during their 120-minute reading block. One hour was spent in whole-group instruction with the classroom teacher, and one hour was spent in small-group instruction, where the small-group instruction is made possible by having almost every staff member in the school teach a reading block. While some grades are having their hour of whole-group instruction, others are having small-group time, and then they switch, which maximizes the number of instructors available for small-group instruction. This allows small groups to be approximately four to nine students to every teacher, where "teacher" can mean instructional aide, all of whom are trained in the school's Open Court reading curriculum. As detailed in Chapter 6, another part of this strategy is to pair the students struggling the most with the reading curriculum with the most highly qualified teachers.

This multiage grouping approach is supported in the broader literature as the most effective way to group students for instruction at least in the early elementary grades (Gutierrez & Slavin, 1992; Mason & Burns, 1996; Mason & Stimson, 1996; Pavan, 1992; Veenman, 1995). Such schools also gave benchmark assessments often, every eight to nine weeks, and regrouped students as a result, so the initial grouping was not set for the year and also did not impact grouping in other subjects, that is, they did not "track" students.

After the first few years of its reform, Kennewick provided additional help to struggling students in the afternoon on the basis of the theory that the greater the academic learning time, the more likely it would be for struggling students to learn to proficiency. Since Kennewick had made reading proficiency the highest priority for the district, they were comfortable with reducing time for elective classes for those students who were struggling to read proficiently and could benefit from extra reading instruction in the afternoon.

The Talent Development High School, and other middle and high schools as well, including Park Middle School in Kennewick, provided many struggling students with "double" periods of math and reading—one period of regular instruction and a second period to provide more targeted assistance. The second period of academic help was provided at the expense of an elective course, usually in art or music or career or technical education. The rationale was that the basic building blocks for learning in all areas were reading and mathematics, and if a student needed more help in these subjects, providing that help was more important than providing the elective class. As described in Chapter 6, an important part of this strategy was ensuring that these double periods of reading and math instruction did not just offer students more of the same but rather were staffed with teachers skilled in additional instructional approaches for reaching students who do not understand the material the first time they encountered it.

Another strategy was for teachers to use lunch periods and their planning and preparation periods to provide even longer, 90-minute time blocks for collaborative planning on the curriculum and instructional program; the exact strategies are described more in Chapter 5 on reallocation to support professional development, but this was another way of using time in the school more efficiently, effectively, and strategically.

Reducing Primary Grade Class Sizes to 15

Another strategy that we include in this section on using time more efficiently is lowering class sizes to 15 in kindergarten through Grade 3. If nothing else, this approach meant teachers could provide more individualized instruction to a smaller number of students in their reading classroom, and it was somewhat easier to take the formative assessment data for a group of 15 students, as compared to 20 or 25 students, and design a coherent instructional plan based on the results. But when combined with cross-age grouping by achievement level, it allowed for even more targeted teaching, as all students in each class would be on essentially the same reading level.

Reducing primary grade classes to 15 in Grades K–3 was a goal for nearly all elementary schools we studied and it was accomplished in many different ways. Madison initially dropped class sizes to 15 via resource reallocation; over time, this was aided by a new state program[2] that provided $2,000 for each Title I eligible student if the district pledged to provide class sizes of 15 in Grades K–3. Kennewick accomplished this goal by having all licensed staff in the school teach reading during the 90-minute language arts period. Indeed, for some schools, Madison adopted this strategy as budget limits have constrained its ability to keep class sizes at 15 the entire day. Columbus Elementary in Appleton and Franklin Elementary in LaCrosse also used both local and state funds to reduce class sizes to 15.

Although there is a loud debate across the country on both the costs and effects of reducing class size as a strategy for boosting performance, we simply report that the schools we studied did seek to implement this strategy. Furthermore, Miles and Frank (2007) also found many high schools that reduced class sizes through resource reallocation. Though debated in the policy and academic communities, for a variety of reasons, most schools and districts seek to reduce class sizes at all grade levels. This strategy and ways to finance it are discussed in more detail in the next chapter. We also note here, however, that the school finance adequacy model discussed in Chapter 7 is resourced at a level to allow class sizes of 15 in Grades K–3.

Summary Comments

Although not everyone will agree on all the strategies implemented by these schools to use time during the school day in different and what for them became more effective ways, the point of this step is that those schools and districts took what was a "fixed" resource—the six hours of instruction during the regular school day—and created multiple strategies for using that time better, including class size reduction at least in elementary schools. In this way, they used a resource more efficiently as the fixed resource now was used to produce a higher level of student achievement outcomes. The examples show that schools and districts, even being educational organizations, can think of doing business in more efficient ways.

STEP 7: EXTENDING LEARNING TIME FOR STRUGGLING STUDENTS

As Chapter 1 illustrated, nearly all the districts and schools provided multiple extra-help strategies for students struggling to achieve to proficiency or even higher performance standards. Some of these strategies are also ways of using time more effectively, and thus, some were mentioned in the previous section. These extra supports reflect a strong American value of giving multiple opportunities for its citizens to accomplish certain goals, in this case, learning to a rigorous performance standard. But these extra-help strategies also reflect a long-held theory of learning, namely, that given sufficient time, most students can learn to high standards (Bransford, Brown, & Cocking, 1999; Cunningham & Allington 1994; Donovan & Bransford, 2005a, 2005b, 2005c).

The strategies combined represent the concrete ways these places varied extended-learning time but held performance standards constant. Extra help and time was provided during the regular school day and year, outside the regular school day, and outside the regular school year, all reflecting many of the recommendations of the Commission on Time and Student Learning and a recent report from the Education Sector (Silva, 2007).

Time During the Regular School Day

Middle and high schools provided double periods for students struggling generally in mathematics or reading and language arts. Indeed, in most of the middle and high schools, reading was provided as a separate subject in addition to a language arts class because large numbers of students entered the schools reading below grade level. Again, the extra reading class was deemed more important for the long-term success of the students than an elective class.

Schools at all levels also provided individual and small-group tutoring during the regular school day. Indeed, research shows that individual and very small-group tutoring is one of the most effective—as well as resource intensive—extra-help strategies (Cohen, Kulik, & Kulik, 1982; Cohen, Raudenbush, & Ball, 2002; Mathes & Fuchs, 1994; Shanahan, 1998; Shanahan & Barr, 1995; Torgeson, 2004; Wasik & Slavin, 1993). The strategy is to intervene very quickly for students struggling over some concept in reading or mathematics and to provide intensive additional help so that the student learns the concept rather than waiting and providing a remedial program after performance has dropped. Thus, the first extra-help strategy was one-to-one or other small-group tutoring but not for a group larger than five students. In most cases, the tutors were certified teachers trained as experts in reading; in some cases, trained and supervised instructional aides were used but usually with struggling students in the middle range of achievement.

Tutoring appeared in the Madison, Kennewick, Rosalia, Reading First, and Monroe cases funded with a combination of reallocated resources as well as grants. We should note that there are many types of tutoring strategies, with varying costs, but Wasik and Slavin (1993) documented impacts for Reading Recovery, Success for All, the Wallach tutoring program, Prevention of Learning Disabilities, and Programmed Tutorial Reading, all of which use teachers as the tutors. However, Farkas (1998) showed that if paraprofessionals (instructional aides) are selected accord-ing to clear and rigorous literacy criteria, trained in a specific reading-tutoring program, used to provide individual tutoring to students in reading, and are supervised, then they can have a significant impact on student-reading attainment. Some districts have used Farkas-type tutors for students still struggling in reading in the upper-elementary grades. A more recent study by Miller (2003) showed that such aides could also have an impact on reading achievement if used to provide individual tutoring to struggling students in the first grade.

Time Outside the Regular School Day but Within the Regular School Year

The second kind of extra-help and extra-time strategy was academic help during before school, afterschool, and Saturday school programs. Columbus Elementary School in Appleton actually obtained a 21st Century Schools grant to fund this strategy. Sometimes the programs pro-vided individual tutoring during these periods, and other times it provided more general homework help; the specific organization of the extra help for this extended day strategy varied across nearly all the sites. But it was a component of the extra-help strategies in most of the sites doubling student performance, and is an "extra-help" resource included in the school finance adequacy model discussed in Chapter 7.

Time Outside the Regular School Year

Finally, the last extra-help strategy was summer school, a strategy research shows to be effective if it has a clear, academic focus like reading and mathematics instruction for elementary and middle school students and taking high school courses failed during the regular school year for high school students (Borman & Boulay, 2004; Borman, Rachuba, Hewes, Boulay, & Kaplan, 2001; Cooper, Charlton, Valentine, & Muhlenbruck, 2000). Again, the various schools and districts funded this strategy with a combination of reallocated funds and well as new grants or existing state support for summer school programming. Funds for summer schools are an "extra-help" resource included in the school finance adequacy model discussed in Chapter 7.

Summary

Not all students received all four types of extra-help strategies, and not all districts and schools provided all four. As you will read more in Chapter 6, the schools and districts we studied offered a variety of combinations of double periods, tutoring, extended-day, and summer school extra-help programs. The point is that the places that doubled student performance had a rich set of extra-help strategies, all providing additional time with additional, instructional support while maintaining the goal of having students achieve up to and beyond the proficient or advanced levels of performance.

STEP 8. COLLABORATIVE, PROFESSIONAL CULTURE

Given the collaborative nature of the work indicated by the previous parts of this chapter, it should be no surprise that one result of the multiplicity of activities was a collaborative, professional school culture—what some refer to as a "professional learning community." We would argue that this culture was largely a product of the above activities and not something created by the schools and districts before engaging in the processes to double student performance. However, because the schools and districts engaged in the doubling-performance processes in a collaborative fashion from Step 1, the leaders understood that the way to attain their ambitious goals was to proceed in a collaborative and not bureaucratic manner with the goal over time of developing a collaborative and professional school culture, what is commonly called a "professional learning community" today.

The literature (Newmann & Associates, 1996) defines a professional school culture as one where teachers know and share high expectations for all students; instruction is "de-privatized," meaning that it is public and is publicly discussed, that teachers observe other teachers, and that teachers take responsibility for the results of their actions. The high expectations were created in Step 3, and because of the relentless pursuit of those ambitious goals, the schools and districts we studied had infused the notion of high expectations for all students into the culture of their educational organization.

The development of a common approach to effective instruction is the embodiment of the "de-privatization" of instruction. In the schools studied, instructional practices were not something that were individualistic and private to each teacher. The schools and districts worked collaboratively to create a common, schoolwide, professional approach to good instructional practice, spent time observing each others' classrooms, had experts or instructional coaches help individual teachers deploy new instructional practices in their classrooms, and used large portions of the collaborative discussions of the formative assessment data to determine collectively how to craft instructional units tailored to those data. As a result, instruction was something out in the open, as it was the subject of public and professional conversations and the focus of ongoing professional development. In districts such as Madison, this represented an enormous change from the status quo, but as previously described, the change was largely welcomed by teachers who were hungry for detailed information about how to implement the new district reading program.

Finally, for the third element of a professional culture—taking responsibility for results—in the schools and districts studied, faculties took credit for the student performance changes that that were produced whether they went up or down. When they rose, as all did over time, the faculties believed it was a result of their hard work on the curriculum and instructional program. Yes, it took student effort as well, but it was student effort that emerged from instructional units and experiences designed and implemented by the teachers in the school. Furthermore, when performance did not rise, the faculties went back to the drawing board to determine why and what to change instructionally for that unit the next year.

An excellent example of this was a side comment in the presentation of the principal of Elmont Junior/Senior High School at the 2007 Wisconsin Conference. He said that one year only 89 percent of the students passed a Geography Regents test and in the next breath said, "We obviously had done something wrong." These comments reflect two key points: The first is that the lower scores reflected a mistake the faculty made not something about students, and the second is that an 89 percent passing rate was not good enough, which reinforced the very high performance expectations in the school.

As this example illustrates, the schools and districts we studied believed that all students could learn and that their achievement was the result of hard work by teachers and principals on the instructional program. When performance did not match expectations, they did not say, "Oh, this group of ninth graders was not as smart as last year's." They did not say, "Well, we needed more money" or "We had to narrow the curriculum because of NCLB pressures" or "If we had more parent involvement, the kids would do better." They said they got something wrong in their curriculum and instructional program and worked together to fix it. A principal in Kennewick described the process he puts in motion whenever data from the school's MAP testing reveals a problem with instruction: "I gather up the teachers in the affected grade, point out the problem, and assign them the task of coming up with a solution to be presented to all faculty during the next professional development day previously built into the school calendar."

Finally, we should say that this professional culture included dogged, relentless, and continuous pursuit of a high level of achievement and learning for all students. These staffs authentically worked to leave no child behind. The Madison central office staff person, who reviewed the periodic running records for all students and then had school visits to ask why certain students where not making progress, is one example of this intense focus on working to ensure that each and every student succeeded and no one fell through the cracks. At Franklin Elementary School in Appleton, when data revealed a weakness in student writing, the principal implemented a system where an example of student writing was required to be submitted to the principal, who personally reviewed each writing sample and then approached the classroom teachers of students who were weak writers and made sure a plan was in place to address the problem. The multiple, extra-help strategies also reflect this relentless effort to have all students achieve: if the first dose of instruction does not work, then the school and its teachers will provide a second, third, and even fourth dose to have as many students achieve to the high bars set for them.

All of the schools and districts that doubled student performance produced a professional and collaborative school culture over time. In these organizations, central office staff, school administrators, and teachers all worked together to attain their ambitious, student performance goals.

STEP 9: WIDESPREAD AND DISTRIBUTED INSTRUCTIONAL LEADERSHIP

Step 9 includes strong instructional leadership provided by principals, teachers, and central office staff. In the educational literature, this is often called distributed leadership (e.g., Spillane, Halverson, & Diamond, 2001). What is clear from the districts and schools studied, not only by our team but also by others as well (e.g., Chenoweth, 2007), is that leadership from all levels in the system helped produce the ambitious, student performance results.

In some cases, schools can produce dramatic improvements in student learning on their own, but it certainly is facilitated if there is support from the central office. Furthermore, central office leadership also is needed to move all schools in a district onto the pathway toward doubling student performance. The Kennewick case showed that not only central office administrators but also board members visited each school to launch their process to have every student reading proficiently by the end of third grade. Furthermore, as in other districts, central office individuals need to be involved both to ensure that state-level testing data were made available in a useable format to teachers and administrators in schools and to provide funds for resources schools need to implement their strategies and sometimes also to provide the authority for schools to reallocate site resources for the needs of a new, educational strategy.

At the school level, principals were usually unable to provide all the instructional leadership needed to change the entire curriculum, create and implement a professional development strategy, work with teachers on the analysis of formative assessment data, and provide the classroom coaching teachers need to change their instructional practice. Thus, as indicated in the professional development section, teachers were promoted into roles of instructional coach, curriculum head, induction mentor, or curriculum facilitator to expand, deepen, and intensify the instructional leadership that could be provided at the school. Though the schools and districts had a wide variety of teacher-instruction leadership roles, research is only beginning to show how formal and informal teacher leadership can be most effectively structured (Mangin & Stoelinga, 2008).

In Abbotsford, district and school leaders created an environment of shared decision making at the school level. Whether making decisions about curriculum adoption, scheduling, or class lists, a team of teachers is always involved. The principal believed that it is natural and important to ask for teacher expertise whenever decisions are made. This philosophy of leadership has had an impact on the school culture, creating an environment in which collaboration and conversation are encouraged and supported by the administration. Teachers are encouraged to take on leadership positions, helping one another with practice, deciding on new textbooks, and contributing to the design of the school's reform. The open lines of communication and trust between faculty and administrators help the school make decisions as a community.

This and other cases profiled in Chapter 1 show that many teachers in the districts and schools studied became engaged in a wide range of instructional leadership activities, which not only provided them career advancement but also the opportunity to ensure that teachers were centrally involved in leading the curriculum and instructional changes that were the foundation of the overall strategy to dramatically boost student, academic learning.

Although these findings reinforce the notion that principals in good schools are instructional leaders, we note that principals do not always have to be the person doing the instructional leadership activities. The function of managing the school—that is, scheduling students, dealing with parents, monitoring the budget, fixing the roof and broken toilets, ensuring security, and so on, has to be conducted by someone. If principals do these tasks, then they need to promote teachers into even stronger instructional, leadership roles, which we often observed. On the other hand, if principals wanted to spend the bulk of their time doing instructional leadership, then they need to make sure some individual is responsible for the other, more mundane management aspects of the school, as both the instructional and noninstructional tasks need attention.

The prime conclusion for the schools and districts we studied is that there was a "density" of instructional leaders in these educational organizations: central office individuals who often have the formal authority to lead the system, principals to lead the site, and teachers as instructional coaches, teacher-mentors, grade-level or department-level team coordinators, and/or schoolwide instructional or curriculum facilitators. In part because of the widespread and distributed leadership structures, the result was that there was sufficient instructional leadership in the organization, the organization was able to maintain its course even when certain formal leadership changes occurred, and a collaborative culture emerged because distributed leadership requires strong collaboration across all levels in the system as well as across all content areas.

STEP 10: PROFESSIONAL AND BEST PRACTICES

Step 10 is an element of the process we have not seen mentioned in other studies, though it may have been implicit rather than explicit. But we want it to be explicit. The organizations that doubled performance were highly professional organizations, actively seeking out research evidence about how to improve schools, looking at best practices from other schools and districts, and seeking the top experts on how to provide the best reading, mathematics, science, and professional development programs.

No school or district we studied produced such large improvements in student performance on their own. They reached out to the education community to find the most current and most appropriate curriculum, instruction, professional development, and change strategies for their school. They read the research, they attended conferences, they listened to experts, they benchmarked best practices, and from that cauldron of professional knowledge, they tailored a strategy for their school or district.

Small rural districts like Abbotsford asked for assistance both from their regional service unit and state department of education. Columbus School in Appleton reviewed the research on comprehensive school designs focused on English language learners. Other schools looked for evidence-based reading or mathematics curriculum. The search for the best ideas was broad and deep in most places.

In this context, we are reminded about a school committed to improving performance in one urban district; this school was profiled in a national newspaper. This school decided to create the "Spaulding School" model[3] of improvement. The staff's notion was that if they could create a plan that worked, then others would want to replicate their efforts. On one hand, this represented a first step towards committing to broad-scale change. On the other, this school gave no indication of reading the literature, interacting with experts, or knowing about the best curriculum programs already out there. Their notion was to design it themselves! Not only is the idea of doing it alone unprofessional, but also, even if they had created a program that worked (the Spaulding model), why would they assume that others would look at theirs since they had not looked at other programs that worked?

The fact is that too many teachers and schools work in too much professional isolation and fall short of what they can do because they are unaware of the considerable professional knowledge of school transformation that already exists. The schools we studied that were successful in producing large gains in student learning and reducing the achievement gap in the process did not operate in isolation. They read as much research as possible, oftentimes in professional journals such as *Phi Delta Kappan* or *Educational Leadership* or written in *Education Week,* reached out to experts to give them advice, tapped the expertise of formal groups created to provide technical assistance, and searched for whole-school designs that had worked elsewhere but in contexts like theirs. In the process, they became what we would call professional organizations, deploying as best they could the state of the art professional knowledge.

SUMMARY AND CONCLUSION

In this chapter, we identified 10 important elements of the processes used in the schools that we have studied that produced dramatic improvements in student learning—what we have labeled doubling performance. Schools in urban, suburban, and rural districts, schools with diverse and not so diverse populations, and both small and large schools around the country have been successful in producing quantum improvements in student achievement and in reducing achievement gaps. And the processes used by these schools and districts reflect the 10 elements discussed in this chapter.

Although other authors (e.g., Blankstein, 2004; Chenoweth, 2007) might have a somewhat different set of key processes, the similarities across our findings and those of others are quite high. Even Grubb (2007), who studied how Finland dramatically improved student performance and also closed the achievement gap, found a very similar set of processes, though he also found that the Finns supported small classes, smaller secondary schools, and higher-quality teachers—strategies that have been proposed in the United States but with mixed support. At the same time, Grubb did not find that Finland spent itself toward higher achievement; much was accomplished by reallocating existing resources and targeting any new resources, strategies that also characterized the sites we studied that doubled performance. The point here is that the ways to turn schools around and to dramatically improve student performance are well known. The challenge is to scale up these strategies to more schools and districts.

As noted throughout this chapter, some of the processes for doubling student performance require considerable resources: extensive and ongoing professional development, reduced class sizes, and extended learning opportunities provided through tutoring, extended-day, and summer programs. Other elements of the process require only modest resources: analyzing state test data, setting high expectations, buying new curriculum materials (after they are worked into the regular instructional budget), getting and analyzing formative assessments, tapping the expertise of the profession, and creating a professional, school culture. One strategy entailed using a fixed resource—time during the regular day—more effectively, and thus more efficiently.

The next three chapters show how the resource-intense strategies were funded, sometimes through resource reallocation, sometimes through targeted use of new general resources, and sometimes through special grants. Those chapters are followed by a short chapter that links these resource needs to school finance adequacy, as the evidence-based school finance adequacy model discussed in Chapter 7 provides all the resources needed for the resource-intense strategies detailed in this book.

NOTES

1. This also is a point often made by the Education Trust; if the initial analysis focuses on demographics and family issues, the dilemma is that education systems cannot change those factors. So the analysis should be on performance in school, something the education system is well positioned to address.

2. The Student Achievement Guarantee in Education or SAGE program.

3. A pseudonym.

Reducing
Class Size

As we discussed in Chapter 3, one strategy that schools deployed to use instructional time more efficiently and effectively was to reduce class sizes. This is a resource-intensive strategy that often requires either extensive resource reallocation or an infusion of new money. Thus, this chapter discusses resource use and reallocation strategies schools and districts have adopted to reduce class size in kindergarten through Grade 3 to 15 students per teacher. As most resource reallocation occurs at sites, the chapter begins with a discussion of categories of resources at the school level and how those various categories of resources have fared in general resource reallocation processes. It then addresses evidence on class-size reduction as an effective strategy. It ends with other examples of reallocating resources to reduce class size in the early elementary grades.

RESOURCES AT SCHOOL SITES

Most of any district's budget is spent at the school site. Instructional expenditures constitute an average of 60 percent to 61 percent of districts' budgets; these expenditures include regular instruction, instruction for the wide variety of categorical programs for special students' needs, books, and classroom materials. Site administration represents about another 5 percent. Most maintenance and operation costs are for school sites. Most of instructional and pupil support is provided at school sites. In total, at least 80 percent of most districts' budgets are spent at and within school sites for a variety of services provided directly to students (see Odden & Picus,

2008). Thus, the site budget is a major focus for resource reallocation as it includes the largest portion of the overall, district budget. We begin our discussions of resource reallocation at the site level, but in the next chapter on professional development, we also discuss how central office resources can be reallocated to support more focused professional development.

Of the funds spent at the school site, the majority is spent on personnel. Often, this fact is a barrier to many educators' understanding of the possibilities for reallocating these resources. School staffs, especially all staff with a teacher license, are too often seen as a "given" and not changeable so only nonstaff dollars are considered for reallocation. But as the following discussions show, the prime source of reallocation is staff at school sites.

To analyze how staffing resources are used in schools and the possibilities for reallocating those resources, it is useful to think of a school's staff as being divided among six categories:

1. *Classroom teachers:* Teachers who teach the core curriculum to students for most of each day. Core curriculum is usually defined as reading, writing, language arts, mathematics, science, social studies (history and geography), and in secondary schools, foreign language.

2. *Regular education specialists:* Teachers of subjects outside the core curriculum, such as art, music, physical education, and library in some elementary schools. Core teachers, then, have planning and preparation time during the time students are in elective classes. In secondary schools, this category includes staff that provides electives such as career-technical, business, family and home, and consumer education.

3. *Categorical-program specialists:* Teachers outside the regular education classroom whose salaries are paid largely by categorical-program dollars, including special education, compensatory education (Title I), bilingual/English as a Second Language (ESL), gifted and talented, and other programs for special-needs students. Generally, staffs providing services for children with severe and profound disabilities are not part of any resource reallocation process.

4. *Pupil support specialists:* Professional staff that provide nonacademic support services to students outside the regular education classroom, such as guidance counselors, psychologists, social workers, family liaison, community outreach, and nurses.

5. *Aides:* Paraprofessional staff who provide either instructional support (including working one-on-one with children both within the regular classroom and in resource rooms) or noninstructional support (including clerical tasks and supervising the cafeteria and/or playground).

6. *Other:* Any other staff employed by the school, including clerical, cafeteria, and custodial workers.

Although different, schoolwide educational strategies require schools to create different combinations of staff; the text refers to these six staffing categories to discuss the resource and staffing allocations and reallocations made at the schools studied. We have developed a more detailed way to categorize staff in schools (see Odden, Archibald, Fermanich, & Gross, 2003) and have used it in several studies of use of resources in schools (e.g., Mangan et al., 2007; Odden, Picus, Aportela, et al., 2008); this framework essentially subdivides the above six categories. For ease of discussion, we refer just to the above six staff categories. Because these staffing categories are all linked to different funding sources, the following discussion also attempts to identify which funding sources were tapped as schools reallocated resources to their new educational strategies.

Reallocating Core Classroom Teachers

Core classroom teachers represent the largest staff category in most schools. Most of the funding for regular-classroom teachers derives from local and state equalization aid dollars. For some of the schools in our studies, those dollars arrive at the school in a lump sum to be spent as the school sees fit. Of course, many districts have class-size maximums that dictate the minimum number of classroom teachers they must hire.

For numerous reasons, schools rarely tap this staffing category for reallocation. As we discuss below, a number of schools—including both elementary and high schools—actually increased the number of classroom teachers to reduce class size, usually far below the maximum levels. Indeed, several elementary schools pooled resources from nearly all other staffing categories to support a strategy of reducing class sizes to between 15 to 17 students all day long (Odden & Archibald, 2000; or see http://cpre.wceruw.org and go to school finance case studies).

Miles and Darling-Hammond (1998) studied high schools that did the same thing, provided class sizes of about 18. By also implementing an integrated curriculum strategy, these high schools reduced the teacher-student contact to just 36 students a day (compared to the typical 150 in most, large high schools), thus making the learning environment more personal and potentially more effective. Karen Miles and her colleagues at Education Resource Strategies have designed a Web-based tool called District Resource Allocation Modeler (DREAM). This tool can be used to calculate, using either the default data in the tool or data from your own district, the resources required to change the teacher load as well as the resources required to fund many other research-based strategies. See http://www.erstools.org/Dream/index.cfm for more information.

We have studied four elementary schools that essentially took all the resources from other staffing categories and, like the successful schools in the Austin, Texas, case (Murnane & Levy, 1996), used them to hire additional teachers to reduce class sizes to the low range of 15 to 17. One school in a rural district took this approach. They transformed four teachers, who had been working in pullout resource rooms and also had dual certification in regular and special education, into classroom teachers and used the salaries of four instructional-aide positions to hire two additional classroom teachers. Thus, the school was able to reduce class sizes to 17. Another school in a medium-sized urban district took the funds from three positions that had supported ESL teachers in a pullout format, and together with funds from Title I, gifted and talented, and some discretionary local sources, hired four more teachers and reduced overall class sizes to 17. In a larger urban district in the East, we studied two elementary schools that implemented a variation of these approaches, all for the purpose of reducing class size to the 15 to 17 range.

At the same time, we studied two elementary schools that allowed class sizes to increase somewhat to allow them to fund professional teacher-tutors and full-time instructional facilitators. These schools believed it was more important to have somewhat larger classes (27–28 students) augmented by the intensive help provided by teacher-tutors, than smaller classes (22–24 students) without any tutoring help. The schools' faculties decided that the small negatives from the modest increases in class size were offset by the large positives of hiring tutors and providing substantially more professional development and coaching.

Both of these schools had adopted the Success for All reading program and were strongly committed to the tutoring, professional development, and instructional leadership that was part of that educational strategy. By choosing to fund tutors and an instructional facilitator rather than hiring additional classroom teachers to maintain class sizes at 25 or lower, these schools effectively reallocated resources away from traditional, regular education expenditures.

Miles and Darling-Hammond (1998) found this same phenomenon for two schools that also had adopted the SFA program; the schools' faculty decided that the small negatives from the modest increases in class size were offset by the large benefits of hiring tutors and a full-time instructional facilitator.

Barring these examples, the staffing category of classroom teachers was generally not tapped as a source for resource reallocation. In most cases, if there was any change to the resources allocated to regular classroom teacher positions, it was in the direction of additional resources.

Regular Education Specialists

Staffing resources for regular education specialists generally have not been reduced or used for resource reallocation. Like core classroom teachers, the funding source for this category is local- and state-equalization aid dollars. The reasons for not reallocating these resources have been twofold. First, schools valued the subject matter that these specialists taught and believed for the most part that these subjects required specialists and could not be covered as thoroughly by incorporating them into the regular education classroom. Second, the teacher contract usually required planning and preparation time for classroom teachers, and the regular education specialists provided this time. Thus, regular education specialists were viewed as necessary for fulfilling contractual obligations.

However, as discussed previously, schools found numerous ways to provide teachers with the time they needed to prepare for and engage in the program restructuring required to implement their strategies to double performance. A few of these strategies did not require keeping the same number of specialist teachers to provide planning time. For example, a school could decide to organize some specials classes, such as physical education, into larger classes than those taught by classroom teachers, thus allowing one specialist to provide planning time for more than one teacher during a single class period. Employing such a strategy freed up the funding that had supported specialists without reducing planning time, and one could argue, without compromising student achievement in the core subjects.

This was a strategy used by Madison. Initially, when the district reduced class sizes to 15 for Grades K–3, specialist and elective classes also were reduced. Over time, however, the district raised the specialist and elective classes back to a more normal 24-student level, which reduced the cost of the class-size-reduction policy.

Another school modestly increased the staff in the specialist teacher area, as well as changed the subjects that were taught. Most interesting, this school replaced an art teacher (a subject that they believed could be integrated into the regular education classroom) with a teacher of social skills (a subject they wanted taught to the large numbers of students from poverty backgrounds). A school in another district sought to turn several full-time specialist positions into several more part-time specialist teachers, thus stretching the numbers of teachers and blocks of collaborative planning time that the funds for these positions could support.

In summation, although planning and preparation time for teachers is important, and it may be possible to provide this time more efficiently than is traditionally done at most schools, for the most part, we found that when specialist teachers were part of a school budget, they tended to remain part of a school budget. The only exceptions were when schools created a more efficient strategy to provide the same amount of planning and preparation time for classroom teachers with a different specialist-teacher strategy, such as the two discussed.

Categorical-Program Specialists

The most extensive resource reallocations have been within the area of categorical-program specialists. There are many reasons for this phenomenon, but simply stated, this is the area where schools have the most discretionary money and have been most unhappy with the results of the strategies they had been deploying. There are three, primary funding sources for this staffing category: (1) Compensatory education funding for remedial and resource room specialists who provide assistance to low-income students; (2) Special education funds that pay for the specialists who provide services both within and outside the regular classroom for students with disabilities; and (3) ESL funds for students who need to learn English.

Compensatory Education

Although compensatory education dollars derive from local, state, and federal sources, for most schools the largest source of funding comes from Title I of the federal No Child Left Behind program. In percentage terms, Title I can represent up to 10 percent of school budgets when the concentration of students from lower-income backgrounds constitutes a high percentage of all students in the school.

All five schools in one study (Odden & Archibald, 2000) were able to apply Title I funds to schoolwide programs, but they used their funds in different ways. One school used the resources to help hire more classroom teachers to keep class sizes down. Three schools used the resources to deploy tutors, instructional coaches, and to pay for the professional development that was part of the Success For All design. For these four schools, as well as for other schools engaging in resource reallocation around the country, federal compensatory education resources were instrumental in enabling them to implement their reforms.

Schools also are beginning to alter the use of funds from state pupil weights for students eligible for free or reduced-price lunch and/or who are

Title I eligible, which have amounted to large sums in Minnesota and Illinois. One Minnesota school we studied received almost $1,000 for each student from a poverty background. In the year we studied it, the school was given control over those funds and decided to eliminate two child development specialists and fund tutors and an instructional facilitator instead.

Although it is not true of all schools, in some schools, the level of federal and state compensatory education dollars is sufficient that when reallocated, they can fund a range of expensive, new educational strategies such as those included in the comprehensive, Roots and Wings school design. For an all-low-income school of about 500 students, this design roughly requires two instructional facilitators (one for reading and one for mathematics), four teacher-tutors, a family liaison, and $70,000 for materials and training. In large numbers of schools, reallocated Title I funds covered the bulk of these additional costs. In the schools studied, additional resources came from the reallocation of remedial reading and math resource teachers and instructional aides for the more effective elements listed above.

Special Education

For most of the schools implementing one of the educational strategies that we have described in the book, resources for special education constituted the second largest source of categorical-staffing resources that were reallocated. Special education dollars, which derive from local, state, and federal sources, often fund staff in pullout resource rooms for students with mental or physical disabilities. Many students with a disability require services outside the regular classroom, but some, especially those with mild learning disabilities, can be better served in the regular education classroom. If the decision is made to integrate some of these students into the regular classroom, the funding for the services that are no longer provided outside the regular classroom can be reallocated.

At one rural K–8 school with about 680 students that implemented an inclusionary model and reduced class sizes, almost all of the money formerly spent on pullout programs for special education was reallocated. Five special education teachers, who were dual-certified in special education and regular education, were reassigned to regular education classrooms of their own to reduce class size. One other similarly dual-certified teacher was hired the year the school adopted the inclusionary model because of rising enrollment. In addition, four instructional-aide positions were eliminated to hire two more dual-certified teachers. In total, eight dual-certified teachers took over regular classrooms in an effort to reduce class sizes from 25 to approximately 15, representing a substantial reallocation of special education resources. The school also sought and was granted a waiver to implement this strategy.

At three other schools, a smaller portion of staffing formerly used for pullout special education services were also used differently, again due to the overall education strategy, in this case the Success for All (SFA) reading program. The SFA reading program groups students by reading achievement levels and, by using all teachers for the 90 minutes of language arts, can reduce class sizes to 15. These three schools decided to have a special education teacher teach the reading class for the students who were having the most trouble with reading. In many cases, these teachers were dually certified in special education or remedial reading as well as regular education, so they were able to more easily teach a homogeneous group of students achieving at the lowest levels. The changes made to special education at these schools represent a reallocation of special education resources to the regular classroom. It should be noted that to make this reallocation legal, many students' individual education plans (IEPs) had to be changed to reflect the new methods by which they were being served.

English as a Second Language

Another source of categorical-program dollars with potential for resource reallocation is ESL. Although this possibility only applies to schools with a significant number of students who are English language learners, schools that do have such students often get funding from a combination of local, state, and federal sources. Like compensatory education funds, these funds are often used for pullout programs that are intended to raise student achievement levels. However, a school we studied with a high number of students with limited, English proficiency questioned whether this was the most effective way of serving these students. Our school example below describes how one school reduced elementary class to 15 to 17 by using these ESL and other categorical-program resources for smaller classes for English language learners (ELL) as well as all students.

Pupil Support, Aides, and Other Staff Resources

The pupil-support-staff categories have rarely been reallocated, but we have encountered a few examples where aide positions were reallocated so that more regular classroom teachers could be hired. For example, in Cordell Place, a district profiled in Chapter 2, all instructional aides were reallocated so that additional certified teachers could be hired either to serve in regular education classrooms or as tutors or instructional coaches. Also, as described in Chapter 7 of Chenoweth's (2007) book, Dayton's Bluff Elementary School in St. Paul, Minnesota, traded 13 paraprofessionals and postponed the purchasing of computer technologies to increase the number of core elementary teachers so the entire school could reduce class sizes to 15 to 16 students.

As noted above, sometimes aide positions were traded in for more core classroom teachers, or other elements of a more powerful, whole-school strategy, such as instructional coaches and certified teacher-tutors. But even with these reallocations of aides, the bulk of funds for resource reallocation generally came from the reallocation of specialist teachers and categorical-program teachers and not much change in the pupil support and other nonlicensed staff in the school.

REALLOCATING RESOURCES TO REDUCE ELEMENTARY CLASS SIZE

The primary decision that affects overall school costs and the context within which instruction will be delivered is regular class size—the number of students that are assigned to each classroom teacher. When class sizes are smaller, school costs generally are higher; when class sizes are larger, school costs generally are lower.

Most of the schools we studied in both our resource-reallocation and doubling-performance research began with regular class sizes of about 25 students. This should not be confused with a pupil-staff ratio, which is the ratio of all students in a school to all licensed staff in a school, whether or not they teach a full classroom of students. By class size, we mean the actual number of students assigned to a classroom teacher during a given class period. For most schools, that was about 25. Thus, a school with 500 teachers and actual class sizes of 25 would have had 20 core classroom teachers.

We have studied many schools that reduced class size far below the standard of 25 students. Moreover, reducing class size has been a popular policy issue across the country for over a decade. By 2000, about half the states had enacted class-size-reduction strategies (Odden & Picus, 2004). In 1998, the federal government initiated a strategy to hire 100,000 additional teachers for the nation's schools to reduce class size to about 18 in the early elementary years, though this policy was dropped a couple years later. Wisconsin implemented the Student Achievement Guarantee in Education (SAGE) program, which was a targeted-class-size-reduction strategy; districts received $2,000 per Title I-eligible student in an elementary school if they promised, regardless of the amount of additional funding received, to reduce class sizes in the school to 15 in Grades K–3. As noted in Chapter 1, Madison initiated its class-size-reduction strategy before the SAGE program was enacted and was able to broaden the strategy to more schools with SAGE funds.

Nearly all of the class-size-reduction policies have been inaugurated because of a growing belief that lowering class sizes improves student learning. Although the research findings that support this belief have been somewhat mixed, today most analysts—and policymakers—point to the results of Tennessee's late 1980s class-size-reduction experiment as the substantive rationale for this policy. This experiment represents one of the few, large-scale, randomized, controlled experiments in education. Thousands of K–3-grade students in scores of schools all across the state were randomly assigned to small classes (between 13 and 17 students), regular-sized classes (between 22 and 26 students), and regular-sized classes with an instructional aide. After four years, the results showed that students in the small classes learned more; the effect size was about 0.25 of a standard deviation, a significant though modest effect (Achilles, 1999). The effect was larger for low-income and minority students; some analyses showed that the effect was about twice as large for these students—close to 0.5 standard deviations (Achilles, 1999; Grissmer, 1999). The effects, moreover, continued into middle and high school and even beyond that (Kreuger, 2002). There was virtually no impact for the classrooms with instructional aides.

Most of the schools and districts that we have studied were aware of this study, and for reasons particular to each school, decided to implement a small-class-size policy for students in every grade. For example, one school was a K–2 elementary school with an enrollment of about 360. It reduced its class size to about 16 students in all grades; doing so required it to hire four additional teachers over its regular allocation of 18 teachers. Another school, serving about 700 students in Grades K–8, adopted the same policy for Grades K–5. Because its K–5 student population was 326 students, it needed to hire eight additional teachers over its normal allotment of 11 teachers to provide all teachers with a maximum of 17 students.

Miles and Darling-Hammond (1998) studied two schools that adopted a similar class-size-reduction policy. A special 90-student elementary school with about one-third of students with disabilities reduced class sizes from 25 to about 15, which required two additional teachers. A high school actually reduced class sizes from the normal of 30 in the district to about 18. Achilles (1999) provides several additional examples of schools that reduced class sizes to around 15 students. Finally, we know of an urban district in the Midwest that has decided to reduce the size of all classes in elementary schools with 40 percent or more students eligible for free and reduced-price lunch (i.e., from a low-income family) to 15 in Grades K–2. As in the previous class-size-reduction examples, this district is able to implement this change without raising tax rates.

In short, all of these schools implemented the typically expensive policy of dramatic, class-size reduction by reallocating teacher resources that already were in the school—that is, without additional funds. The remainder of this chapter describes the details of how they accomplished this extraordinary feat. The purpose here is simply to state that many schools and districts across the country have provided quite small classes in the early elementary grades by using the dollars in their schools differently. It is important to emphasize that these schools provided small classes for all elementary-level teachers for the entire school day: All regular academic subjects were taught to classes of approximately 15 to 18 students.[1]

Still, other schools that we studied only reduced class sizes for particular subjects, mainly reading, which they believed was the most important subject on which to focus their efforts and is the subject for which the research is strongest in terms of the impact of small class size. Two elementary schools provided class sizes of less than 20 for their daily, 90-minute periods of reading instruction by having not only the regular classroom teachers but also several other licensed staff—reading tutors, art and music teachers, and others like these—teach reading during the 90-minute-reading, instructional time block. Two other elementary schools we have studied—one that was profiled in the first edition of this book and one described in Chapter 3, Washington Elementary School in Kennewick, managed to reduce reading class sizes even more for struggling students using existing resources. The first of these examples reduced class sizes for reading below the level of 15 for the lowest-performing students in Grades 1–3. By requiring nearly all licensed staff in the school to teach reading during the 90-minute reading block, this school provided reading class sizes of 10 to 12 for the students having the most difficulty learning how to read. The second example, Washington Elementary, used all available staff (including aides) to teach reading and managed to reduce class sizes to between four and nine students per instructor for one hour of the two-hour reading block each day. As described in Chapter 6, both of these schools assigned the most skilled teachers—with either additional expertise in teaching reading or with an additional licensure in learning disabilities—to work with the classes containing the lowest-level students. This illustrates the kind of smart use of resources that some would argue represents the best chance the country has of meeting the goal of teaching all students to high standards.

Facilities

Of course, a big question that is always raised about a small-class-size strategy is, "Where do the schools find the space?" Generally, this has not a major problem. In some cases, classrooms were divided in two, and teachers taught in teams to effectively share space and make class-size reduction possible. One school was successful in passing a referendum to build a new school to make the reduced class sizes possible. But overall, the schools we studied did not have significant problems finding classroom space—and none were significantly under-enrolled. They simply began using school space differently.

In other cases, school leaders found innovative ways to reduce class sizes. When a new principal was hired at Columbus Elementary School in Appleton (Wisconsin), she was told that although the school was eligible for funds to reduce class sizes to 15 in Grades K–3 through SAGE, the former principal had turned down the funds due to a lack of space. Knowing how critical these small classes were to the success of her students, the new principal refused to take no for an answer. Instead, she rented space from a building across the street, accepted the funds, and lowered class size. She admitted that this was not an ideal situation, to walk some students back and forth across the street, but it was well worth the extra effort in terms of the benefits for students.

Many of the teachers that were reallocated for regular classroom teachers had been using rooms for other purposes, mainly elective classes. Since some of these teacher positions were eliminated, their rooms became available for regular classrooms. For example, if a remedial-reading-teacher position was eliminated, and that position were turned into a classroom-teacher position, that room could be converted to a regular classroom, thus providing space for class-size reduction.

We had thought that implementing smaller classes would be more difficult for small schools. As we indicated above, one of the class-size-reduction schools enrolled just about 360 students. But even this school was able to reduce class sizes to 16. Yes, this required some teachers to share classrooms, and the school had to use all spaces—including the library and lunchroom—more efficiently, but it was able to find the space. In fact, the year this school implemented the class-size-reduction policy, it grew by 40 students so it had to find two additional classrooms. It found even more extra space and still implemented its small-class-size policy.

Let us give you another example of why space might not always be a problem. Recall that we know of a district reducing class size to 15 for its schools with 40 percent or more students qualifying for free or reduced-priced lunch. Initially, the district concluded there was insufficient space. But on further analysis, they found that a "used" classroom was a space for one teacher. The room was considered "used" even when the students were gone from the classroom for their "specialist" classes, which occurred at least once, and sometimes twice, during the day. The classroom was unused during lunch. In this district, teachers had a full afternoon off each week for additional planning time, and the room was considered "used" during that time as well. In short, a "used" room was used only about 65 percent to 75 percent of the time. The district decided to increase that closer to 100 percent. In part, they were able to do so by having the art and music teachers "travel" to the classroom for the specialist classes, thus freeing up art and music rooms.

The above are just examples of ways schools and districts found space. These examples illustrate that each school that decided to reduce class sizes somehow found the space to do so. To be sure, the strategy would be harder but not impossible for a growing school with all rooms fully used. The Columbus Elementary example showed how one school found the space by renting it from a building across the street. Similarly, as they began reducing elementary class sizes in the late 1990s, many districts lacked the necessary space to reduce class size. Often, the solution was for schools to lease portable classrooms. The leasing strategy allowed them to provide small classes quickly rather than waiting the long time for the capital construction money required to construct additional, permanent classrooms.

SCHOOLWIDE STRATEGIES TO REDUCE CLASS SIZES

This section includes examples of schoolwide strategies to reduce class size—one from a medium-sized, Midwestern district and two from a larger, more urban Midwestern district. These more detailed descriptions of how schools reallocated resources to reduce class size illustrate the trends described in the first part of this chapter in terms of what gets reallocated to reduce class size and what does not.

Farnham

As mentioned in Chapter 2, Farnham Elementary, one of the schools profiled in the first edition of our book, used a creative strategy for financing their class-size reduction. We describe it in more detail here because it illustrates the principles discussed in this chapter.

Farnham Elementary School is located in a medium-sized urban district in the midwestern United States. The school serves only Grades K–2 because it is paired with another elementary school serving Grades 3–5. The student population of approximately 360 students is about 38 percent minority. Approximately 23 percent of all students qualify for ESL services, and 35 percent qualify for free or reduced-price lunch.

The principal at Farnham was largely responsible for instigating change. First and foremost, she was concerned about the school's low achievement scores: Farnham was one of 29 elementary schools in a district of 45 schools, and its students consistently scored in the lowest quarter of all elementary schools in the district. Second, the principal was concerned with the school's practices of pulling students with special needs out of the classroom for extra help. This included Title I, ESL, and special education students; none of whom were having much academic success in their current program. The principal at Farnham chose to address this concern over student learning by virtually eliminating pullout programs, such as ESL small group instruction and Title I remediation, and using those staff slots to hire classroom teachers to reduce class size to approximately 16. Both the principal and the teachers believed they would be better able to serve all students in these smaller, more inclusive settings. In this way, she also managed to improve the continuity of the instructional program and to increase the number of minutes all students spent on reading.

To achieve the desired reduction in class size, the number of regular classroom teachers had to be increased by six. The resources to pay for those positions were largely reallocated from categorical funds that had been paying for all of the pullout programs. These included 5.1 positions in all: The 1.1 Title I teacher, the 3.0 ESL teachers, the 0.4 minority-achievement teacher called "RISE," the 0.2 gifted and talented teacher, and the 0.4 supplemental-teacher allotment were all reallocated to pay for regular classroom teachers. The school gained an additional classroom teacher because of an unexpected increase in enrollment for a total of seven additional classroom teacher positions.

The school organized teachers into a series of two-teacher teams, each with about 32 to 34 students. Some of the groups were multiage (usually spanning two years), and some were the same age. Moreover, nearly all teams had two adjoining classrooms that usually had an open wall between them. Finally, during reading, each team organized reading groups from all students in the two-teacher-team grouping.

We should note that because this school had a low-income student population of only 35 percent, the principal had to obtain a waiver to use Title I funds for schoolwide purposes rather than the pullout program. Predicting that she would need additional money for the intensive professional development that was necessary to help ensure quality implementation of the school's new educational strategy, the principal also applied for and received a Comprehensive School Reform (CSR) grant in the amount of $62,000. This money helped support that staff development—much of it focused on developing ESL teaching skills for all teachers as described in the next paragraph.

To accommodate students with special needs in the regular classroom, most of whom were ELL students, teachers needed to learn instructional strategies that would help them simultaneously teach content as well as language development, the latter a need for about one-third of the students in most classrooms. By offering classes in ESL instruction at the school site, the principal addressed this need with an intensive professional development program. This concentrated use of resources for professional development, approximately $15,000, was paid for with the money from the CSR grant. This was six times the amount of money spent on school-site professional development in the previous year. In using professional development dollars to give teachers additional skills, one of the resource-allocation strategies employed at Farnham was to shift some of the functions that had been provided by the teachers who formerly taught in pullout programs onto regular education classroom teachers.

Although the principal's goal was to have all the teachers dual-licensed in regular education and ESL, she recognized that this could not happen immediately. Therefore, she began by making sure there was at least one, dual-certified teacher on each teacher team for the 1998–1999 school year and encouraged all teachers who were not dual certified to enroll in the professional development program. The principal then implemented a policy of only hiring teachers with dual certification to allow the school ultimately to have only dual-licensed staff for all teaching positions.

To make these changes at Farnham, the principal had to win the support of the superintendent and school board in her community. Although she was able to persuade them, she had to agree to have her students' achievement closely monitored so that the district could be sure that Farnham's new educational strategy was working. One condition of the district's approval was the submission of a yearly report by the school on students' academic performance under this program. The district also made a requirement that the principal make a yearly presentation to the school board on the implementation and effect of the program on Farnham students. Last, the award of the CSR grant was contingent upon the submission of a yearly report monitoring student progress. With the support of these agencies contingent on the results at Farnham, the principal had to be very specific in her plans for the assessment of the inclusionary class-size-reduction model.

The main assessment being used to monitor student progress was a district test, the Primary Language Arts Assessment (PLAA). These district tests are aligned with the state's list of academic standards, which is an outline of what students should know and be able to do by the fourth, eighth, and twelfth grades. As these tests are administered to young children who are just beginning to read and write, the format of the test includes a reading portion as well as a "Words I Know" section, where students write as many words as they can in a specific time (three to five minutes).

However, because so many of the students at Farnham did not take the PLAA in the 1997–1998 school year, there were no baseline scores with which to compare the 1998–1999 scores. Therefore, the principal devised a system whereby the 1999 scores would be compared to the benchmarks set up by Reading Recovery, a program designed to help children who are struggling with reading. Ambitious goals were set for 1999 according to those benchmarks, and those goals were that 95 percent of first- and second-grade students would read at grade level as measured by Text Reading Level (TRL) of 16+ for first graders and 20+ for second graders. Although the school did not meet these goals in the first year—60 percent of first graders scored a TRL of 16 or higher, and 88 percent of second graders scored a 20 or higher—the principal found these scores encouraging as many more students were hitting the benchmark than had in the previous year. Furthermore, many more students (mainly ELL students) who were previously excluded from the test took it this year, a victory in itself according to the principal. But the most important measure of the success of the new strategy comes from the results of the state third-grade reading test at the partner elementary school. In November 2002, 84.5 percent of students scored at the proficient or advanced level. Although this is short of the principal's goal of 95 percent, there is no question that the changes she made at Farnham were positive for its students.

Clayton and Parnell

These two schools were located in a large urban district in the Midwest. They are both K–8 schools with 300 to 400 students, with about 95 percent of the students eligible for free and reduced-price lunch and African American. Both schools had been low-performing schools—prior to NCLB—and were reconstituted in 1999 by a joint, eight-member teacher union and school administration team. The team first selected a whole-school design for each school, then selected the principal, and then with the principal selected lead teachers. The principal and lead teachers then selected all remaining teachers for the school. Furthermore, each school selected specific, new curriculum programs that aligned with their whole-school designs and vastly expanded professional development. In addition, each school became one of the first schools in the district to move to a school-based budgeting system, funded by what today is called a weighted-student formula.

Both schools also adopted a small-class-size strategy to reduce classes at all grade levels to 15 to 20. Although going beyond what the research would support as a class-size-reduction strategy for just Grades K–3, these schools nevertheless decided to reduce class sizes across the board. Clayton needed eight, additional teacher positions from the normal allocation to reduce its class sizes. To accomplish this goal, the school did the following:

- Eliminated 12 aides to hire four teachers
- Eliminated one pullout special education teacher for the fifth teacher
- Used a federal class size reduction grant for the sixth teacher
- Used the reconstitution augmentation to fund the seventh teacher
- Allocated an additional budget augmentation to move to school-based budgeting for the eighth and final additional teacher (being one of the first schools to do so)

In summation, the school tapped resources from several different areas to fund what would have been considered a class-size policy that was unaffordable. This example shows how its strategy of small class sizes included not only resource reallocation but also strategic allocation of additional dollars that could be used for any purpose.

The other school, Parnell, needed to hire nine additional teachers over the normal core-teacher allocation. It accomplished this goal both by reallocation and strategic allocation by doing the following:

- Eliminated five instructional aides to hire two teachers
- Reallocated Title I money for the third teacher
- Used federal class size reduction funds for the fourth teacher
- Used the district's reconstitution fund budget augmentation for the fifth teacher
- Hired four new teachers for Grades 7 and 8 while only two would have been needed for regular class sizes

As such, Parnell also is an example of both targeted-resource reallocation and strategic allocation on general dollars.

A DISTRICTWIDE STRATEGY TO REDUCE CLASS SIZE IN EARLY ELEMENTARY GRADES[2]

The Kenosha Public School District in southeastern Wisconsin was faced with a number of different, educational, and fiscal challenges in the late 1990s. A medium-sized urban district in the Midwest, Kenosha serves a growing population of approximately 20,000 students. Demographically, its student population was 77 percent white with 11 percent Hispanic, 9 percent African American, and 2 percent other. Hispanics represented the largest and fastest growing minority group. About 30 percent of Kenosha's students lived in families with incomes below the poverty level, as indicated by eligibility for the federal free and reduced-price lunch program. In the previous decade, the percentage of students from low-income backgrounds continued to grow.

But rather than being evenly distributed across all schools, many of the district's low-income, minority, and limited-English-speaking students were concentrated in a small number of its schools. The concentration of educational challenges that usually accompany these demographic characteristics made it more difficult for students in these schools to achieve the high standards set for them by the state and the district. Although a growing student population combined with a generous state education aid program helped ensure budgetary stability for the district, the district nevertheless began to struggle more and more to find the fiscal resources required to deploy programs successful in boosting the performance of its low-income and minority students.

In an effort to meet the achievement goals for all students over the 1990s, the district began to implement a number of education-reform initiatives. These included a number of curriculum reforms, reconfigurations of schools into K–8 campuses, full-day kindergarten, and smaller classes in Grades K–3, beginning first with the schools with the highest concentrations of students from poverty backgrounds. The issue was how to finance the latter two resource-intensive initiatives.

Leaders in the Kenosha School District in Wisconsin managed to significantly reduce class size in the majority of their elementary schools—through the use of creative resource reallocation and deployment of all the revenues made possible by student demographic characteristics and the state's school finance system. By 2000, more than one-third of Kenosha's elementary schools had class sizes of 18 or lower, and all 24 schools had class sizes at or below 22. Individual schools in this district had begun to reduce class size school-by-school by reallocating federal Title I and VI funds, a state compensatory education program, and using SAGE. But the districtwide goal of getting all elementary class sizes to 18 or lower and to expand kindergarten from half- to full-day could not have been funded with just categorical-dollar reallocation.

The major revenue source for this expensive policy was excess revenues derived from the combination of growing enrollment and the shift from a half-day to a full-day kindergarten. For every new student that enrolled in the district or for every two students who moved from a half-day to a full-day program, the marginal cost of educating that student(s) was approximately $3,000, but the district received an extra $7,000 via the state school finance formula, or an excess of average, over-marginal costs of $4,000 per child. The total combined district enrollment growth from these two phenomena—natural growth and kindergarten expansion—was about 500 students a year. This produced excess revenues of nearly $2,000,000 (500 students times $4,000 per student), which was sufficient to hire 40 additional teachers at an individual cost of $50,000 in salary and benefits. This quite ingenious way to fund smaller class sizes, combined with additional dollars from selected categorical programs—federal Title I, Title VI, state SAGE, and P5[3]—allowed for even lower class sizes in the highest-poverty, lowest-performing schools. Thus, the district reached the level of 18 or lower in nine of its 24 elementary schools.

This case shows how important it is for district leaders who want to make changes using reallocated dollars to have full knowledge of the district budget and how that budget is derived. In Kenosha, district leaders decided to reallocate categorical dollars to class-size reduction, but they needed an additional source of funding to reduce class sizes to target levels. They were able to find that additional funding source because they understood the principle that "new" students, whether from natural enrollment growth or the shift from half-day to full-day kindergarten, could produce "new" dollars because of the excess of average, over-marginal costs. These changes enabled the district to provide full-day kindergarten and reduce class sizes in all elementary schools, initiatives that research shows are particularly powerful in helping students from low-income backgrounds learn to read and do mathematics in the early elementary grades (McRobbie, Finn, & Harman, 1998; Slavin, Karweit, & Madden, 1989; Slavin, Madden, Dolan, & Wasik, 1996).

SUMMARY

This chapter has given some examples of how schools and districts can reallocate (and in some cases allocate) resources to reduce class sizes. In some cases, schools reduced class sizes all day and for all grades; in other cases, class sizes were reduced only for reading or only for Grades K–3. While there is research to support class-size reduction as a strategy for improving student achievement (Achilles, 1999; Grissmer, 1999), we do not mean to suggest that it is necessarily one of the steps to doubling performance. We merely cite these examples and note that many of the schools that have reduced class size have also doubled performance—the relationship is not necessarily causal.

Also, as Miles and Frank (2007) point out, a small-class-size strategy is more effective when teachers receive professional development around how to teach smaller groups of students effectively. In the next chapter, we discuss in more detail just how critical professional development is to doubling performance and give examples of how schools and districts have found the money to fund it.

NOTES

1. Miles and Frank (2007) provides examples of high schools that also have reduced class size, often to the 18-to-20-student level.

2. More details of the Kenosha approach are included in Odden and Archibald (2001a).

3. P5 is a small state program to provide extra funds for elementary schools enrolling large numbers of students from poverty backgrounds.

Finding Resources for Professional Development

This chapter addresses the very important issue of professional development, the resources needed to provide a professional-development program that works, and various strategies for finding the resources to financially support a vigorous, ongoing, professional-development set of activities, which are key to making any strategy to improve student performance work. As stated at the end of the previous chapter, our perspective is that funding a comprehensive, ongoing, professional-development strategy—including the important school-based coaches—is the key to success with many, individual strategies, such as class-size reduction. Thus, it should be the top priority for any district or school launching a strategy to dramatically boost student performance.

This chapter has four sections. The first section details the resources needed for a solid, effective, and comprehensive professional-development strategy. Section 2 describes what we have developed and called a professional-development, fiscal, and program audit—a strategy that analyzes how much districts currently spend on professional development, the purposes of those expenditures, and whether current practices align with the new directions in which the district and its school want to move. Section 3 provides examples of reallocation at the district level to fund professional-development programs, and the final section gives school examples of reallocation to finance ambitious professional development.

RESOURCES NEEDED FOR AN EFFECTIVE PROFESSIONAL-DEVELOPMENT PROGRAM[1]

Effective professional development is defined as professional development that produces change in teachers' classroom-based instructional practice, which can be linked to improvements in student learning. The emerging consensus on what characterizes "high-quality" or "effective" professional development draws upon a series of empirical research studies that link program strategies to changes in teachers' instructional practice and subsequent increases in student achievement. These studies include, among others, the long-term efforts of Bruce Joyce (Joyce & Calhoun, 1996; Joyce & Showers, 2002), research on the change process (Fullan, 2001), a longitudinal analysis of efforts to improve mathematics in California (Cohen & Hill, 2001), Elmore's study of District 2 in New York City (Elmore & Burney, 1999), the Consortium for Policy Research in Education's longitudinal study of sustained professional development provided by the Merck Institute for Science Education (Supovitz & Turner, 2000), studies of comprehensive professional development to improve science teaching and learning (Loucks-Horsley, Love, Stiles, Mundry, & Hewson, 2003), and an evaluation of the federal Eisenhower mathematics and science professional-development program (Garet, Birman, Porter, Desimone, & Herman, 1999).

In summarizing the key features of effective professional development, we and others (e.g., Elmore, 2002; Joyce & Showers, 2002; Odden et al., 2002) have identified six structural features of such programs:

1. The *form* of the activity, that is, whether the activity is organized as a study group, teacher network, workshop, mentoring collaborative, committee, or curriculum development group. The above research suggests that effective, professional development should be school based, job embedded, ongoing, and focused on the curriculum rather than just a one-day workshop.

2. The *duration* of the activity, including the total number of contact hours that participants are expected to spend in the activity, as well as the span of time over which the activity takes place. The above research has shown the importance of continuous, ongoing, long-term, professional development that totals many hours annually—(i.e., at least 100 hours and closer to 200 hours).

3. The degree to which the activity emphasizes the *collective participation* of teachers from the same school, department, or grade level. The

above research suggests that effective professional development should be organized to include the *entire faculty.*

4. The degree to which the activity has a *content focus,* that is, the degree to which the activity is focused on improving and deepening teachers' content knowledge, as well as how students learn that content. The above research concludes that effective professional development focuses on the content of the curriculum—including problems students typically have learning that content—and effective instructional strategies for that content.

5. The extent to which the activity offers opportunities for *active learning,* such as opportunities for teachers to become engaged in the meaningful analysis of teaching and learning—for example, by scoring student work or developing and refining a standards-based curriculum unit. The preceding research has shown that professional development is most effective when it includes opportunities for teachers to work directly on incorporating the new techniques into their instructional practice with the help of instructional coaches.

6. The degree to which the activity promotes *coherence* in teachers' professional development by aligning professional development with other key parts of the education system such as student content and performance standards, teacher evaluation, school and district goals, and the development of a professional community.

Form, duration, and active learning together imply that effective professional development includes some initial learning in training sessions (e.g., a 10-day summer training institute), as well as considerable longer-term work in which teachers incorporate the new methodologies into their actual classroom practice. Active learning implies some degree of coaching during regular school hours to help the teachers incorporate new strategies into their day-to-day instructional practices. It should be clear that the longer the duration and the more coaching, the more time is required of teachers as well as professional development trainers and coaches. Content focus means that effective professional development focuses largely on subject matter knowledge—what is known about how students learn that subject—and the actual curriculum that is used in the school to teach this content. Collective participation implies that the best professional development includes groups of and at some point all teachers in a school or district, who then work together to implement the new instructional strategies and in the process build a professional school community. Coherence suggests that the professional development is more effective when the signals from the policy environment (federal, state, district, and school) reinforce rather than contradict one another or send multiple, confusing messages. Coherence also implies that professional-development opportunities should be given as part of implementing new curriculum and instructional approaches. Note that there is little support in this research for the development of individually oriented professional-development plans; the research implies a much more systemic approach that involves all teachers in the school.

Each of these six structural features has resource requirements, as summarized in Chapter 3. Form, duration, collective participation, and active learning require various amounts of both teacher and trainer/coach/mentor time during the regular school day, year, and, depending on the specific strategies, outside of the regular day and year. This time costs money. Furthermore, all professional-development strategies require some amount of administration, materials and supplies, and miscellaneous financial support for travel and fees.

In summary, the resources needed to mount a long-term, professional-development program that is effective in changing teachers' instructional practices require the following:

- Time during the summer for intensive training. This upfront training can most easily be accomplished by ensuring that approximately 10 days of the teacher's normal work year are pupil free and dedicated to training and professional development.
- On-site coaching to help teachers incorporate the practices into their instructional repertoire.
- Collaborative work with teachers in their schools during planning and preparation periods to improve the curriculum and instructional program, thus reinforcing the strategic and instrumental need for planning and preparation time during the regular school day. This will require smart scheduling of teachers during the regular school day and week.
- Funds for training during the summer and for ongoing training during the school year, the cost of which can be estimated at about $100/pupil.

A PROFESSIONAL-DEVELOPMENT FISCAL AND PROGRAM AUDIT[2]

To determine how much a district or school is now spending for professional development, we have developed a cost framework for professional development (Odden et al., 2002), and we have used this framework, along with tools created by Karen Miles (Miles, Odden, Archibald, & Fermanich, 2004), to estimate actual expenditures on professional development in several large districts. The cost framework shows that professional-development programs require six types of resources:

1. Teacher time for training, usually in full or half days. This time can be provided by extending the teacher contract to provide training during the summer before school starts or providing pupil-free days during the regular school year. The latter strategy, however, often means students receive instruction from a substitute teacher, which is not ideal. The cost is the stipend or daily rate teachers receive for the extra days during the summer and/or the cost of substitute teachers during the school year.

2. Time during the regular school day and year for collaborative planning. This is possible when districts provide teachers with planning and preparation periods, during which specialist teachers provide instruction in elective classes. Core classroom teachers then have pupil-free time. Schools and districts then need to claim a substantial portion of this time for collaborative work by teachers on the curriculum and instructional program.

3. Trainers. Whether provided by central office professional-development or curriculum support staff or by outside experts and consultants, districts and schools need resources to pay the fees and/or the salaries for the individuals who provide the training.

4. Instructional coaches. These are the individuals who work with teachers in their classrooms and help them incorporate new instructional strategies into their ongoing instructional repertoire. Instructional coaches are the critical key to having professional development lead to change in instructional practice.

5. Administration. A small amount of funding is needed to organize and administer comprehensive professional-development programs.

6. Miscellaneous resources for supplies (coffee and donuts), materials, and reimbursement of tuition and conference fees if those are part of the overall professional-development program.

We and others have used this framework to determine how much districts are actually spending for professional development, because after the need for substantial, ongoing professional development is realized, the next question is how to pay for it.

More and more educators and policymakers have concluded that significant resources are needed for intensive professional development designed to enhance teachers' instructional expertise. We agree with this claim. But the most typical clarion call is that *more* resources are needed to finance these professional-development services. In many districts, this claim may not be true; substantial resources could be found by reallocating extant resources already being used for various professional-development activities.

Indeed, after analyses of the actual level of professional-development spending in many large urban districts, research using the professional-development, fiscal-audit tool is beginning to show that, at least in many of these types of districts, the issue is less the need for more money for professional development and more the need to recognize the extant large investment in professional development and to reallocate those funds to more effective professional-development strategies.

The professional-development resources we summarized above and in Chapter 3 can be translated into an amount-per-pupil in 2005 of roughly $450, detailed as follows:[3]

- $42 per pupil for 10 days over the work year for intensive training[4]
- $311 per pupil for placing instructional coaches in schools at the rate of one coach for every 200 students[5]
- $100 per pupil for trainers, whether central office professional-development staff or outside consultants

This clearly is a substantial amount of money for school districts, and such amounts are rarely shown in any professional-development budget.

District Spending on Professional Development

However, using this professional-development, fiscal-audit tool, we have shown in several large urban districts that they were spending this level of money on various professional-development activities. In a five-district study, Miles et al. (2004) found that the per-teacher amount varied from $2,100 to $7,900[6] just from district sources. Translating these numbers into rough, average per-pupil numbers—based on a staffing model of 30 teachers in a 500-student school—the amount spent on professional development ranged from $70 to $263 per pupil just from district sources. In one urban district, moreover, professional-development investment from school level sources (separate from district sources) doubled the amount per pupil from $228 to $501 (Fermanich, 2003), sufficient to cover the ambitious professional-development resources suggested above. These studies also showed that very little of the professional-development spending was focused on improving instruction in the core academic subjects (mathematics, science, reading/writing, history/geography), further eroding the impact of the expenditures on boosting student achievement in these subjects.

The message from these studies is that large urban districts should first do a professional-development, fiscal, and program audit of their extant professional-development strategies before deciding whether additional funding is required. It could very well be that what is required is a reallocation of their current professional-development expenditures to strategies focused on improving teachers' instructional practice in teaching the core academics. This type of ambitious resource reallocation to fund new and ambitious professional-development programs was the foundation of the effective program in New York City's District 2 (Elmore & Burney, 1999), led by then superintendent, Anthony Alvarado.

Alvarado and his central-office staff dramatically expanded professional development by eliminating most of the categorical-program and instructional-support staff in the central office and turning the funds supporting those positions into dollars for professional development (see Elmore & Burney, 1999). The district eliminated nearly all district-level program support staff for federal (Title I) and state compensatory education programs and bilingual education and reduced the amount of money used for special-education program support. It took those funds and reallocated them to professional development—instructional coaches, summer institutes, and trainers—focused on reading, writing, and mathematics. Over a five-year period, the district expanded professional-development expenditures to about 5 percent of its operating budget. It then used those funds to focus relentlessly on developing teachers' instructional expertise in reading. After that period, the district's students produced some of the highest ever scores on the New Standards Reference assessments.

Alvarado was subsequently hired as a superintendent of instruction in San Diego. Hightower, Knapp, Marsh, & McLaughlin (2002) details the restructuring that took place in San Diego to refocus the district on teaching and learning, as well as the resource reallocation necessary to fund the new, ambitious, professional-development strategy. The main programmatic components were 300 peer coaches (at a cost of approximately $87,500 per coach), $5,000 for every first-grade classroom to purchase new materials, and additional learning experiences for students and staff after school and in the summer. A total of $62 million was reallocated for the 2000–2001 school year, which was 6 percent of the operating budget. These funds were taken from a number of different sources, including $19 million from Title I, $16.6 million from integration funds, and $15 million from state funds for school libraries and new-teacher induction. An additional $6.2 million from a redesign of central administration was dedicated to the peer coaches. In the following school year, approximately $96 million was spent on this redesign strategy from similar sources of reallocated funds. The bottom line: This district was able to reallocate sizable funds to powerful instructional strategies.

We should note that this kind of resource reallocation is not easily accomplished. Jobs were eliminated, practices were changed, focus was provided, and millions of dollars were reallocated. These changes are good examples of performance management. But Hightower et al. (2002) also describes the controversies surrounding these changes and the difficulties of implementing the strategies for reallocating resources to fund needed professional development.

Although it may be possible for large urban districts to find substantial professional-development expenditures that potentially could be reallocated, suburban and rural districts might have more trouble finding enough money to reallocate, particularly if the district does not receive large amounts of categorical funding for students in poverty. Research findings on existing professional-development spending in large urban districts should not be generalized to suburban or rural districts. We are not aware of any professional-development fiscal and program audits that have been conducted in suburban districts. However, a study of one rural district in Wisconsin found that, other than a double-planning and preparation period for middle school teachers, similar levels of professional-development spending did not exist, and any ambitious, professional-development program would require additional funds (Thayer, 2004).

Nevertheless, before seeking more money for professional development, we would urge all districts to first conduct a fiscal and program audit of their existing professional-development strategies. Doing so might help them uncover resources that could be better used for a revised professional-development strategy focused on implementing new curriculum programs.

School-Level Reallocation to Support Professional Development

As stated above, in the one district where we conducted a professional-development fiscal and program audit at the school level, seeking to find school-level resources devoted to professional development over and above those provided by the district, we found that school spending equaled district spending, thus doubling professional-development expenditures found from just the district audit. Thus, we would encourage all schools to scrutinize their budgets for professional-development resources that could be deployed more strategically.

Indeed, in our resource reallocation research, we found many schools that redeployed teachers from certain roles to instructional-coach roles. Many schools have moved Title I reading teachers into instructional-coach roles, working individually with classroom teachers to help them incorporate new instructional strategies, usually for reading and mathematics, into their ongoing repertoire. We also have found many elementary schools that have traded their certified-library position for an instructional-coach position, by putting an aide in the library and automating the circulation system for library books.

DOUBLING-PERFORMANCE DISTRICTS

We were not able to determine the exact resource reallocation strategies for many of our doubling-performance districts and schools. (Where these details are available, we share them below.) However, we note that they all expanded professional development, added many additional days of training, put instructional coaches into schools to help teachers use the new instructional strategies, and somehow found the funds to pay for the needed training. In some cases, new money was needed to pay for these strategies.

For example, Abbotsford's procurement of a READS grant included funds to dramatically expand professional development for teachers. Grant funds were used to purchase the time necessary for teachers to learn how to use the new curriculum. The principal was able to pay for substitute teachers so that teachers could participate in off-site training, visit other schools already implementing the new curriculum, and work in grade-level teams to strategize about lesson planning together. Finally, the grant made it possible for a literacy coach to spend considerable time in the school modeling, observing, and providing feedback to teachers using the curriculum for the first time.

In interviews, leaders expressed their views about the problems inherent in providing one-shot training for teachers. They described the importance of extensive, professional development in new curriculum to prevent teachers from simply returning to the old, comfortable way of doing things. The grant allowed the school to invest in extensive, new professional development, which supported the successful implementation of the new curriculum, as well as instructional improvement. Many of the schools we studied in Washington funded these strategies with their Reading First funds as well.

Madison also implemented an induction program for new teachers so that they too received sufficient training to begin implementing the district's new reading program. By expanding the number of teachers each year who were provided professional-development opportunities in the district's new reading program, Kennewick made systemwide professional development an ongoing priority.

District and School Resource Reallocation to Fund Professional Development, Instructional Coaches, and Teacher-Tutors

Emerging research on what is being done in schools that are dramatically improving student performance includes examples of schools that have reallocated resources to fund these powerful strategies. For example, the Donaldson School in Chattanooga, Tennessee, which improved student performance as part of the Benwood Initiative, reallocated $180,000 in Title I money, taking funds that had been used for pullout instructional aides and reallocating the money to support lead teachers as coaches and to pay for other training expenses related to their intensive professional-development program (Chenoweth, 2007).

From our own work in Rosalia, one of the districts profiled in Chapter 1, one of the budgetary decisions that staff made was to make professional development a priority by reallocating resources to pay for training. That district cut back on maintenance, food service, and secretarial staffing to fund ongoing professional development at a high level.

In Monroe, another of the districts profiled in Chapter 1, the new curriculum director knew the vital importance of professional development in supporting changes to classroom instruction and realized that school-based instructional coaches were the key—although expensive—factor that could significantly impact change in classroom, instructional practices that would be linked to student learning gains. Coming up with the money to fund school-based instructional coaches meant reallocating district and Title I resources to provide instructional coaches to each elementary school instead of licensed math tutors during the first year of implementation. The curriculum director provided the rationale for and research on the effects of instructional coaches and convinced the administrative team that school-based instructional coaches were necessary to support teachers during implementation to help them integrate into their ongoing classroom practice the strategies they were beginning to learn through professional-development sessions on *Everyday Math* in the summer prior to implementation. Another key element was common planning time for teachers to have collaborative discussions about mathematics instruction.

This and the other professional development necessary to prepare for and implement the new curriculum are summarized below:

1. Introduction to New Program/Textbook:
   - One-half day inservice in spring 2002 (one and one half hours of state department of education math consultant overview of math education, one and one half hours *Everyday Math* consultant)
     Cost to District: $2,000 *Everyday Math* consultant, including mileage and hotel, plus teacher time, included in the contract
   - One-day inservice in August 2002 with *Everyday Math* consultants
     Cost to District: $300 for consultant, plus teacher time, included in the contract

2. Planning/Collaboration Time:
   - One-day inservice in August 2002 for planning and collaborating with grade-level colleagues
     Cost to District: teacher time, included in the contract
   - Two hours per month per grade level for meeting and common planning time
     Cost to District: $6,318, not included in the contract

3. Additional Support:
   - One differentiation and follow-up inservice with *Everyday Math* consultants regarding how to meet the needs of all students in the classroom
     Cost to District: $4,000 ($1,500 for Grades 3–5; $1,000 for Grades 1 and 2; $750 for kindergarten, plus mileage and hotel)
   - Three instructional coaches (one per building)
     Cost to District: $180,000 ($60,000 per coach for salary and benefits)
   - Three-day training in Chicago for instructional coaches
     Cost to District: $1,500 × 3 = $4,500

Total Cost (for one year), excluding teacher time already in the contract: $197,118

Another powerful example of reallocating resources to fund powerful professional-development strategies came from one of the districts whose change process was described in Chapter 2. As you will read in the next few paragraphs, in Cordell Place School District, the district and school worked together to fund a new school strategy, the professional development that needed to accompany implementation, as well as teacher tutoring that was part of the new school strategy. Hollister Elementary School (not its actual name) is a kindergarten through fifth-grade school serving approximately 511 children in Cordell Place School District, a suburban district in the northwestern United States. The student population was approximately 49 percent minority. About 6 percent of the students received special education services, and about 3 percent received instruction in English as a second language. Approximately two-thirds of the students were eligible for free or reduced-price lunch.

For many years, Hollister's students were among the lowest achievers in the district. The staff at Hollister found it increasingly difficult to teach the increasingly low-income population of students that attended their school and began looking for a new and more effective curriculum. At the same time, a new superintendent came to the district, a man who shared Hollister's (and other schools') dissatisfaction with the persistently low achievement scores. The superintendent of this district decided to initiate change by making an offer to all schools with more than 50 percent low-income students. This was the deal: If the school would undergo a year of self-study to identify the nature of their performance problems and identify an evidence-based new curriculum program and school vision, then the school would be given full control over its Title I budget to use for the chosen strategy. (This self-study, described in Chapter 2, was also very similar to the first step in the ten steps toward doubling performance.) To ensure that the Title I money the schools received would be viewed as discretionary, the superintendent declared that all Title I, remedial-reading teacher and instructional-aide positions would not exist the following school year. Instead, the Title I money used to fund those positions would be part of the lump sum of Title I money given to the schools that underwent the self-study and could be deployed for any need within their new educational strategy.

Low reading scores were judged the most pressing problem by the Hollister staff, so the research-based strategy they selected was a reading program called Success For All (SFA). Implementing SFA (one of the more expensive reading programs on the market) required substantial reallocation of the school's resources. The main elements of the program are extensive professional development, including a full-time instructional facilitator or coach, at least one licensed teacher to serve as a reading tutor (plus 1 more full-time tutor for every 100 students in poverty), a full-time family liaison, and SFA reading materials. The instructional facilitator and tutors were new expenditures for the school, and the professional-development program and instructional materials (then about $50,000 and now about $70,000 for a school of 500 students) required dramatic increases in the amount of money the school spent for those purposes. The following paragraph describes how Hollister found the money to fund the program.

The professional development required for this program was extensive and involved not only programmatic spending but also paying travel costs and hiring substitutes for teachers when they had to attend seminars. In addition, the school had to purchase special instructional materials for the program. In total, the school spent $35,000 on SFA-related professional development and materials; $12,000 of Title I funds were used to pay for the SFA contract, $14,500 of the state reading grant funds helped cover the costs of professional development, and $8,500 from a combination of Title I and the state reading grant funds were used to pay for the required instructional materials.

With the superintendent's elimination of the Title I, remedial-reading teacher positions from the school's Title I budget, Hollister had funds for two teacher positions. The school used these funds to pay for the full-time, instructional coach and the licensed teacher-tutor. Even if the superintendent had not made the decision to eliminate all Title I specialists, this would have been the most logical area from which to shift resources because the implementation of SFA eliminated the need for these resource-room teachers. Still, it was probably easier for the school to make such a change because the superintendent did not give them a choice of using those funds the way they had been used.

Because Hollister had such a high percentage of low-income students, SFA recommended they hire two additional teacher-tutors, but the school could not find the money to do so. Instead, they used 13 hours a day of instructional-aide time for one-on-one tutoring. The aide time used to provide tutoring was funded by a combination of Title I and a state reading grant that the school was awarded in the year that they implemented the SFA program. Although these aides had previously been employed at the school, using them to provide tutoring rather than to provide classroom support and funding them with Title I and grant funds rather than the general allocation represented a shift in the way those resources were being used. While it is true that research has shown that aides performing the role of tutor are not as effective as licensed teachers (Shanahan, 1998), the school felt that making this resource shift was the best they could do to fully implement the program. To cover the functions of the family liaison position required by the model, the school was able to use a position already in place, a full-time guidance counselor. To do this, the role of the counselor was expanded to include the family outreach and social-services-coordination functions embodied in the Success for All family liaison position.

Cordell Place School District and Hollister Elementary School put a comprehensive testing program in place to monitor and help ensure improved student achievement in the wake of these reforms. In the

1996–1997 school year, the California Test of Basic Skills (CTBS) scores were at 33 percent for reading and 27 percent for math. The following year, 1997–1998, they rose to 46 percent in reading and 51 percent in math. In 1998–1999, the CTBS was not administered. Instead, the third graders were given the Iowa Tests of Basic Skills (ITBS) in April, and their scores on that test were 49 percent for reading and 49 percent for math. On the state achievement test given in April of 1997, the reading score was 33.3 percent, and the math score was 3.9 percent. The next year, in April of 1998, the reading score increased to 43.3 percent, and the math score rose to 15.2 percent. In 1999, the reading score dropped a bit to 39.7 percent, and the math score fell slightly to 13.4 percent. Even with these slight dips, the results represent substantial improvement.

While these scores have not yet reached the statewide averages of 48 percent in reading and 22 percent in math, they have increased significantly. The principal credited the SFA reading program and its accompanying Math Wings program with having "made all the difference in the world." She described parents as being excited about the program as well. And, she emphasized that without the commitment of the staff to these initiatives that resulted from the yearlong needs assessment, the school would not have seen such improvement. Much of this was possible through resource reallocation.

USING EXTANT PROFESSIONAL-DEVELOPMENT DAYS EFFECTIVELY

One common theme across districts and schools managing to dramatically improve student performance is that they use the pupil-free days that already are in the teacher contract for a very specific professional-development purpose: to improve core instruction. These student-free days are almost always built into teacher contracts, though the number of days varies from state to state and district to district, from a low of about 1 day to a high of about 15 (in some of the wealthier districts we studied in Washington). Because teacher time is expensive, this represents a significant amount of resources currently allocated for professional development. However, these days are too often a part of the scattershot approach many districts take to providing professional development, rather than a resource targeted toward improving instruction in the district. They are often used for motivational speakers, teacher union meetings, and training unrelated to core instruction.

In the doubling-performance districts and schools, these days are used to present information to staff that is directly related to their instructional-improvement strategy. When Monroe implemented its new math curriculum, these days were devoted to training teachers on that curriculum. In Rosalia (Washington), these days have been used to become more familiar with the content of the state test and to work together on how they can improve in targeted-content areas. At Washington Elementary School in Kennewick (Washington), some of these professional-development days are controlled by the school and some by the district (this is the case for many districts). When the school-controlled, professional-development days are approaching, the principal analyzes formative assessment data for the current students and identifies possible gaps or weaknesses in teaching for a specific subject or grade. The principal then brings this information to the staff directly involved, for example, the fourth-grade teachers, and asks that they devise (with his assistance) a plan for this day that will help these teachers move forward and strengthen their instruction where necessary. This approach ensures that these days are used to help the district reach their goal of getting 95 percent of students reading at grade level.

PLANNING AND PROFESSIONAL-DEVELOPMENT TIME

One of the most fascinating aspects of the research on school restructuring and resource reallocation has been the varied and comprehensive approaches all schools have adopted to provide planning time for teachers as part of new, extensive, professional-development strategies. Although this component of school operations often gets shortchanged in many schools and districts, the schools studied took this issue seriously and invested extensive resources in it.

First, all of the schools studied, both in the reallocation research and in the doubling-performance research, employed additional teachers in specialist, elective subjects to release core classroom teachers for planning, preparation, and professional development during the regular school day.[7] This strategy generally required the schools to hire 20 percent more teachers. So, for example, if a school had 20 classroom teachers, they hired 4 additional teachers. At this level of additional staffing, each classroom teacher was provided approximately one period, generally about 60 minutes a day for every day of the week, for planning and preparation time.

Generally, these specialist teachers provided instruction in art, music, and physical and library education. When students had these "specials" classes, the regular classroom teacher was released from instructional tasks during that time. Although the subjects taught by the specialist teachers tended to emphasize the traditional special subject areas, there also was variation. For example, one school with discipline problems hired a social-skills teacher instead of an art teacher.

One reason it is not too surprising that schools reallocating other resources did not change their use of specialist teachers is that the school faculties considered the specials class subjects—art and music—as important in their own right and were unwilling to merge them into the classroom instruction for the more academic subjects of reading, writing, mathematics, science, and social studies. Another reason is that the planning time provided by those teachers—one period a day, five days a week, for every classroom teacher—was required by the teachers' collective-bargaining contract. Although there may be other ways to provide this planning time, the schools we have studied have generally kept their specialist teacher positions.

Of course, providing some time during the school day for planning and preparation is just Step 1 in providing the time necessary for successful implementation of these new school strategies. Step 2 is to schedule that time in a way that allows teachers to work together, a topic addressed next.

Finding Blocks of Time

A question that is almost always raised about schools engaging in program restructuring, resource reallocation, and doubling student performance is how teachers find the time to engage in all of the instructional and noninstructional decision-making, collaboration, and professional-development activities. A part of the answer to that question is given above: Most of the places studied had specialist teachers on staff who, when they taught elective classes, also provided teachers at least one period a day each day of the week for planning, preparation, and potential collaborative activities on curriculum and instructional issues. But most of the schools did more than just provide this time. They then increased this time and scheduled it more effectively using a variety of strategies.

First, many schools scheduled all teachers on the same teams for the same free period. This included teams of grade-level teachers in elementary schools and teams of content teachers in secondary schools. This allowed the teachers to meet and engage in various activities as a team. Some of the scheduling was incredibly creative for schools where teachers were part of two or three different decision-making teams. Grade-level teacher teams might be scheduled for common planning time two days a week. Then, content teams (math, science, etc.) might be scheduled for a common time on a third day, leaving time for other teams to be scheduled for common time on the other two days. Furthermore, the most effective schools were very clear that the agendas for each team had to be attended to, thus not letting student discipline problems or other subjects dominate all of the team meetings.

In some cases, when time for grade-level team meetings was not a part of the school schedules, other arrangements were made to ensure that teachers had this important time to collaborate. For example, in Monroe, district leaders knew that adopting a new math curriculum required regularly scheduled, grade-level team meetings for the teachers for two hours per month—an essential piece of ongoing professional development. Because the teacher contract did not include time that could be used for such purposes, district leaders decided to pay teachers an additional stipend to ensure that teacher meetings around instruction took place. After the first year of implementation of the new math curriculum, each building principal built collaboration time into the school day. The amount of collaboration time varied by grade level and building, but the intent was to continue discussing how to best meet the needs of all the students.

Second, schools devised many additional strategies to provide teachers more time for collaboration during the regular school day. One common strategy was to have teachers extend the school day for 30 minutes for four days and then release the students for two hours in the afternoon of the fifth day, which provided an extended period for planning, preparation, and professional development. This type of strategy requires parent sanction and cooperation from the district, especially in situations where students are bussed to and from school. It nevertheless is a strategy widely used across the country—and it does not require additional resources! This approach provides all teachers two hours of uninterrupted planning time once every week and at no additional fiscal cost.

Madison has implemented this strategy for years, releasing elementary teachers from instruction for about two hours every Monday but has not lengthened the school day for the other four days of the year. In this way, the district provides schools two hours of possible collaboration time one day of every week in addition to the regular planning and preparation-time periods.

Another strategy is to have teachers voluntarily begin school an hour before students arrive or remain at school for an hour after students leave. Yes, this represents additional time, but the teachers in such schools simply said that the job they wanted to accomplish required this extra time. Even though they might have a period free each day and sometimes even a free afternoon, they said the ambitious restructuring they were involved in could not be done within that time constraint. This willingness to spend extra time collaborating on curriculum, instruction, and data-based decision making also suggested that teachers saw real value in spending their time in these activities; it helped them to be better and more focused in their classroom instructional activities.

Some schools devised even more creative ways to carve out the time teachers needed for collaborative work. One high school did two things that provided significant teacher planning and preparation time. First, students had a block of free time each day to engage in extended self-directed study. During these study periods, they were not supervised by a licensed teacher. Second, students in the same school were required to perform service activities and engage in learning activities off the school campus—that is, in different locations around the community. Again, not all of these ventures were directly supervised by a licensed teacher. Both of these components of the instructional program released teachers from instructional responsibilities and provided time for them to engage in planning, preparation, and professional development. This additional time was especially necessary because this school was implementing a complex, integrated-curriculum program that required this type of intensive planning. Therefore, by finding a way to provide these extensive time blocks to teachers, the school did what it needed to do to implement their new, curricular strategy.

Another elementary school in an urban Midwestern city set a goal to provide 90 minutes of uninterrupted planning time for each teacher team four days each week. This district is not a high-spending district, so the goal was ambitious. Moreover, the school also increased student-instructional time, making the scheduling of the 90-minute planning time even more complex. An explanation of how the school planned to provide this preparation time follows.

First, prior to the new plan, students were scheduled for classes for six hours each day, where as teachers were scheduled for seven hours. This structure provided 60 minutes of free time each day for teachers. This time, combined with a planning period during the day, could have provided the time for the 90-minute planning block with some creative scheduling. But the school did not choose to do this because part of their new, educational strategy was to extend the students' instructional time by one hour per day. To provide the additional hour of instruction, the school changed the student schedule to 8:00 a.m. to 3:00 p.m., the same as the teachers', thus eliminating that built-in hour of preparation time.

Next, the school set aside 8:00 a.m. to 1:00 p.m. as an uninterrupted, academic instructional block each day. Instruction in reading, mathematics, science, and social studies was provided during these five hours. Teachers and students then had lunch from 1:00 p.m. to 1:30 p.m. After that, all classroom teachers had 90 minutes of planning time from 1:30 p.m. to 3:00 p.m. The most creative part of the schedule was how the school planned to provide this free time for all classroom teachers each afternoon.

The school took three full-time specialist-teacher positions, which was part of its regular budget, and converted them into 10 part-time positions at 0.3 full-time equivalent (FTE) for each part-time position. The plan was to have the 10 part-time teachers provide all of the supervision and instruction during the afternoon time from 1:00 p.m. to 3:00 p.m. In addition, because a teacher at 0.3 FTE works for 2 hours and 15 minutes per day, these teachers were also in charge of making sure students got on the buses between 3:00 p.m. and 3:15 p.m.

Of course, it does not work for both the teachers and the students to begin their day at 8:00 a.m., so the school required teachers to arrive at 7:45 a.m. instead. The school then compensated teachers for that extra time by allowing teachers to leave at 1:45 on Friday afternoons, while still allowing them the four, 90-minute blocks of planning time each week.

However, the school was unable to implement the plan fully because they could not find the 10 part-time teachers. Nevertheless, the plan shows how it might be possible for a school to provide these large amounts of planning time and also extend the student's instructional time by an hour each day—without spending additional money.

Another elementary school in a large, Midwestern city wanted to provide a 90-minute planning block to each grade level five days each week. Their strategy was to schedule the normal planning period either right before or right after the teacher's lunch time. Although this required teachers to eat during their 90-minute planning block, the teachers decided that this was a small price to pay for the benefit of a very long, uninterrupted block of planning time.

But, as was the case with the other school that tried to schedule 90-minute blocks of planning time, this school was not able to implement this schedule for a number of reasons. First, if specialist time for each grade level was provided the same time each day, the plan would allow only two grade levels to have the common planning time backed up with lunch— one grade with the specialists covering their classes before lunch and another after lunch. Second, if the grade levels were to rotate having specials backed up with lunch, the school could not meet the goal of providing five 90-minute blocks of planning time for every grade level each week.

Therefore, the school had to compromise its original goal and implement a plan that provided each grade level at least one 90-minute block of planning time a week, with a specialist covering one of the two periods backed up with the teachers' lunch. This strategy, however, required each grade to have specials classes at different times each day during the week. Initially, this was viewed as problematic, as teachers felt elementary students liked and needed a consistent daily schedule. But as the plan was implemented, the school discovered that students were easily able to handle the differing daily schedule.

Another school in the same district was able to implement a 90-minute planning period backed up with lunch for each grade level by scheduling lunch at different times for different grade levels. For Grades K–1, lunch was from 11:05 a.m. to 11:45 a.m. and the planning period from 11:50 a.m. to 12:35 p.m. For Grades 2–3, lunch was from 11:50 a.m. to 12:35 p.m. and the planning period from 12:40 p.m. to 1:20 p.m. For Grades 4–5, lunch was from 12:40 p.m. to 1:20 p.m. and the planning period from 1:20 to 2:10 p.m. In this way, every grade was able to have a 90-minute planning period when teachers decided to use lunch for this purpose.

We should note that the latter two examples are derived from research conducted by Karen Hawley Miles and Linda Darling-Hammond (1998) and that the district was a strong, union district. We also should note that teachers in the school proposed this schedule and use of lunch, which was beyond what was required by their union contract. But the teachers placed a high priority on long, uninterrupted planning periods and were able to find the time by using free time and specialist-provided time creatively.

In short, schools devised numerous strategies to provide significant time for planning, preparation, and professional development (see also Office of Educational Research and Improvement, 1996). In all the instances we have studied so far, faculties were helped in this creative process by having specialist staff already included in the regular school budget; these positions provided at least one period (30 to 55 minutes) of planning time each day during the week. Through creative scheduling, teachers were often able to find even more time for these important tasks. When asked whether it was worthwhile to give up their lunch period, nearly all teachers said some version of, "Yes, this does represent my having to use time for planning that was previously a free period, but the time expenditure is worth it because it has helped us make great strides with student performance."

SUMMARY

The main points to take from this chapter are that funding a comprehensive, ongoing, professional-development program is key to producing large improvements in student learning, and the funding and time needed for such new, professional development can often be found within current budgets and within current time constraints. When implementing a professional-development strategy, districts and schools need to ensure that the programs provide teachers (and other staff when appropriate) sufficient days of training, provide schools with a sufficient number of instructional coaches to work one-on-one with teachers until they can incorporate new, instructional strategies into their ongoing repertoire, and pay for the trainers necessary to provide the training. Without these resources, the professional-development program might fall short of being effective.

Before seeking additional funding, we would suggest that districts and schools first conduct a professional-development fiscal and program audit, using the cost framework we have developed. As this chapter has shown, often districts already are spending large sums of money on professional-development activities that are a mile wide and an inch deep, not focused on the core-curriculum areas, and which produce little if any positive impact. If this is the case, the current strategies need to be eliminated, and the resources redeployed to professional development that is focused on the new curriculum and instructional program—which is sustained over time and includes the school-based instructional coaches needed to produce change in teachers' instructional practice.

Finally, schools and districts also need to use traditional planning and preparation time more creatively. These blocks of time should not be considered the private domain of teachers for a "free period." They should be considered system resources that schools and districts, through focused and creative scheduling, can use to provide teams of teachers the time for collaborative work on the curriculum and instructional program, and thus, give professional development the characteristic of "job-embedded."

It could very well be that more resources for professional development are required. The Madison case showed that the district had some yet insufficient resources to place instructional coaches in all schools. And most of the doubling-performance cases found some resources for instructional coaches but not sufficient resources to work on improving student performance in all subjects or at all schools. But the requests for more professional-development resources should come after the professional-development fiscal and program audit, so that both current and any new resources are used for strategies that are comprehensive, fully developed, and focused on the core content areas of reading, writing, mathematics, science, and history.

NOTES

1. This section draws heavily from Odden and Picus (2008), Chapter 4.
2. This section draws heavily from Odden and Picus (2008), Chapter 7.

3. This amount will vary by class size, provision for planning and preparation, and other factors but is a good, medium estimate of what an effective professional-development program would cost.

4. Based on the National Education Association (NEA) average teacher salary rate for 2005 of $47,808, 205 contract days per teacher or a daily rate of $233; we add here the cost of five additional days at $1,166 and divide that by the average number of teachers in an average-sized school (500/18) for an additional $42 per pupil.

5. Based on the NEA average teacher salary for 2005 and a benefit rate of 30%, for a school with 500 students, it would cost $155,376 to hire 2.5 coaches, or $311 per pupil.

6. When expenditures for contracted professional-development days are not included, the per-teacher amount ranged from $2,100 to $5,000.

7. We should note that all teachers in schools, including those teaching specialist classes, have planning and preparation periods.

Funding Extra-Help Strategies

When schools and districts undertake an instructional-improvement process, one of the areas that inevitably demands attention is strategies for students struggling to meet the standards. Although the last few decades have seen an increase in the funding for students who need extra help, many of the strategies used to serve these students have not been effective. For at least the past twenty years, studies of the effectiveness of bilingual education—programs supported under the Federal Title I and similar state, compensatory education programs, as well as programs for students with disabilities—have found that educational effects have been meager (e.g., Borman & D'Agostino, 1996; Odden, 1991; Reynolds & Wolfe, 1999; Slavin et al., 1989; Vinovskis, 1999). The schools studied had become increasingly frustrated with the results of these traditional strategies, which included some version of service in a resource room, usually focused on remedial reading or mathematics. When students were provided extra help in their regular classroom, an instructional aide rather than a licensed teacher usually provided it, and that instructional aide was usually not trained nor provided the same professional development as the teachers in the school. In a few cases, students had access to computerized instruction of basic skills. None of these strategies were producing the desired results.

In the current policy context of No Child Left Behind and its requirement that achievement of subgroups of students be reported separately, schools can no longer afford to have ineffective strategies in place for serving struggling students. One of the methods of addressing this issue has been to include these students in the regular classroom and focus on increasing the quality of classroom instruction through the use of professional development. Although this is of critical importance and of greater benefit to these students than the previous service model, the reality is that even with the best classroom instruction, some students will need additional time and help to learn to the level of rigorous performance standards.

In this chapter, we discuss three of the most promising extra-help strategies supported by research and being implemented in the districts where performance is improving dramatically: individual and small-group tutoring, additional academic help before and after school, and summer school. Some of the supports we have discussed earlier in this book, including small-class sizes, also helped the schools we studied manage to raise the achievement of students at all levels, particularly those at the lowest level. But the focus of this chapter is on the use of tutoring, extended-day instructional time, and summer school. Where possible, we give examples of how resources were reallocated to fund these practices.

This chapter has three sections. The first section focuses on providing tutoring to students needing extra help during the regular school day. The second section discusses providing extra time during the regular school day/year for students struggling to learn reading and math, which can take the form of an afterschool or extended-day program or a "double" period of reading and/or math. The latter is more common at the middle and high school level, where it typically involves trading an elective class for another class period of reading and/or math. The third section of the chapter is dedicated to summer school.

INDIVIDUAL AND SMALL-GROUP TUTORING FOR STRUGGLING STUDENTS

Research suggests that individual and small-group tutoring is one of the most effective strategies for boosting student performance (Cohen et al., 1982; Cohen et al., 2002; Mathes & Fuchs, 1994; Shanahan, 1998; Shanahan & Barr, 1995; Torgeson, 2004; Wasik & Slavin, 1993). The same research tends to show that students benefit more when tutored by certified teachers, but there is also some research that suggests that when aides are trained, they too can be effective tutors to struggling students (Farkas, 1998; Miller, 2003). Certified teacher-tutors are needed the most for students in the bottom quartile with more complex learning struggles; trained paraprofessional tutors would be best used for students in the middle quartiles with less-intensive learning issues. The districts and schools we studied that doubled performance used both strategies successfully, as described in the next few paragraphs.

In our reallocation research, many of the elementary schools studied reallocated resources away from their traditional remedial-reading strategies to the support of teacher-tutors who worked with students on an individual basis. In most cases, a tutor (sometimes including two individuals each tutoring for half the day) would spend about 20 minutes a day with each of the 12 to 15 students, providing them with one-to-one tutoring in reading. Furthermore, it was the students in Grades 1–3 who received the vast bulk of the tutoring service.

Through our school finance adequacy work in Washington, we learned that the schools involved in the Reading First program received funds for two tiers of intervention—30 minutes of small-group (three to five students) tutoring for students with mild struggles and an additional 30 minutes of small-group tutoring for students with more complex difficulties. Most of the instructors for these extra-help interventions were licensed teachers, but in some cases, they were specially selected, trained, and supervised paraprofessionals.

In one Washington district, Rosalia, that doubled performance (and was profiled in Chapter 1), interventions for struggling students were based on a three-tier model. The first tier was the teacher instructing all students from a common curriculum. The second tier concentrated on small groups of one to five students who were given a second dose of the content. The third tier was largely one-on-one with an aide all day long. Every effort was made to identify struggling students early so that they could be moved from the first tier and placed in the second or third tier depending on their needs.

For the second tier, which included the small-group instruction in literacy, the schools used paraprofessionals to help get the ratios of instructor to students so low. Many of these paraprofessionals were certified teachers who either had not yet found teaching positions or preferred to work fewer hours and chose to be paraprofessionals. All paraprofessionals, regardless of their educational background, were treated and trained just like teachers with the same level of professional development. This strategy was effective for the district and required fewer resources than it would if only certified teachers were used to provide the small-group instruction.

Even so, the district was only able to afford these strategies because part of their philosophy for helping struggling students to succeed was to concentrate resources on Grades K–3. In this way, Rosalia reallocated resources to pay for tutoring, using resources that previously went to middle and/or high school students that were targeted to the early elementary grades. In addition, the district had a policy that instructional aides could not be used for putting up bulletin boards or making copies, which were functions they had performed in the past. This change was also, in effect, a reallocation of resources used for paraprofessionals, away from administrative functions and toward instructional activities.

At Washington Elementary School in Kennewick (Washington), which was also profiled in Chapter 1, small-group instruction was used as a strategy for ensuring the success of all students. It was part of the school's explicit strategy for helping the lowest-level students learn to read. During the two-hour literacy block at the school, for one of the hours, all students received small-group instruction in reading. The lowest-level students received this instruction from certified teachers, many of whom had advanced knowledge about teaching reading (such as a master's degree in that subject), in ratios of 4:1 or 5:1. This strategy was made possible, in part, by the school's use of paraprofessionals—who, like their colleagues in Rosalia, were used to teach literacy and trained to do so with the same professional development provided to teachers. By using paraprofessionals to teach the middle 50 percent of students (in terms of their level of achievement), the most knowledgeable and experienced teachers were free to work with the students needing the most help in very small groups.

In Abbotsford, both Title I and English language learners (ELL) funding were used to provide tutoring for at-risk students, so those needing extra support received some tutoring services during the regular school day. This funding was central to providing sufficient tutoring resources to students, but the principal explained that with more funding, he would be able to offer more tutoring, thus supporting the growing population of ELL students more successfully.

At Columbus Elementary School in Appleton (Wisconsin), teachers used formative assessments to identify the students needing tutoring the most. During the regular school day, formative assessments helped teachers identify students in need of extra help, and those students were assigned to work with the Title I reading specialist in a tutoring capacity. First graders also worked with tutors from a district program called United for Reading Success, in which volunteers were trained to work one-on-one with students struggling to learn to read. The principal at Columbus worked hard to organize the resources from the district and Title I to pay for tutoring because she knew how fundamental it was to her students' success.

Another example of the use of tutoring comes from Houston in the late 1990s when the district used both teacher-tutors and paraprofessional tutors to help struggling students succeed. In addition to implementing the Success for All (SFA) program in about 80 of its elementary schools, which included teacher-tutors for students struggling to read in Grades K–3, the district developed an additional tutoring strategy for students that were still struggling in Grades 4–6. The upper-grade tutors were trained instructional assistants and not fully licensed teachers. But the district followed the procedure developed by George Farkas (1998, 1999) who designed an effective instructional-aide-as-tutor program that we referenced earlier in this chapter. Every aide serving as a tutor had to meet a stringent literacy requirement—that is, they had to be educated and literate themselves, and they underwent a multiple-week training program in a specific tutoring curriculum. These paraprofessional tutors were closely supervised while they were tutoring the upper elementary grade students.

As is shown in the examples above, some schools acquired grant funds to pay for tutoring while some allocated other funds, such as Title I, to pay for this strategy. In any case, as the research suggests, using funds to tutor struggling students during the regular school day was a powerful part of the extra-help strategy used in the schools that doubled performance.

We should also note that many of the schools we studied for the first edition of this book reallocated their resources to pay for tutoring as part of the comprehensive school designs they adopted. In two cases, schools chose to increase class sizes slightly in order to fund professional teacher-tutors and full-time instructional facilitators. These schools believed it was more important to have somewhat larger classes (27 to 28 students) augmented by the intensive help provided by teacher-tutors than smaller classes (22 to 24 students) without any tutoring help. The schools' faculties decided that the small negatives from the modest increases in class size were offset by the large positives of hiring tutors and providing substantially more professional development and coaching.

Both of these schools had adopted the SFA reading program and were strongly committed to the tutoring, professional development, and instructional leadership that were part of that educational strategy. By choosing to fund tutors and an instructional facilitator rather than hiring additional classroom teachers to maintain class sizes at 25 or lower, these schools effectively reallocated resources away from traditional regular-education expenditures.

Miles and Darling-Hammond (1998) found this same phenomenon for two other schools that also had adopted the SFA program; the schools' faculty decided that the small negatives from the modest increases in class size were offset by the large benefits of hiring tutors and a full-time instructional facilitator.

The most common comprehensive school design adopted by the schools we studied for our resource reallocation work was SFA. Although this program suggests the use of certified teachers in the role of tutor, we saw a combination of certified teachers and paraprofessionals used to perform this function. This was often a result of limited funds available to pay for teachers serving in a tutoring capacity. Still, as the research shows, trained paraprofessionals can also be effective in this role, and the school's use of them for this purpose constituted a reallocation of resources from the traditional administrative functions they performed to this role of helping struggling students succeed with the regular curriculum. In addition, including these paraprofessionals in professional development, which had not always been the norm, is another way of using resources to ensure that this position is used most effectively to help improve instruction.

EXTENDED TIME FOR STRUGGLING STUDENTS TO LEARN THE CORE CURRICULUM

As the research suggests and our doubling-performance schools and districts have shown, when given sufficient time most students can learn to high levels (Bransford et al., 1999; Cunningham & Allington, 1994; Donovan & Bransford, 2005a, 2005b, 2005c). Building extra time into the school day during the regular school year is one strategy that helps struggling students keep up with the rest of their classmates and stay on grade level in math and reading. This extended time can take a number of forms—usually, afterschool or extended-day programs but also double periods of reading and/or math. These two strategies are discussed below.

When extra time is provided by extending the school day, it is often as part of an afterschool program. However, extended learning time is distinct from the enrichment activities often provided in afterschool programs because it focuses on instruction in reading and math and is staffed by a certified teacher or teachers. Because they focus on extending the time that students are exposed to these core subjects, these are often called extended-day programs.

Many of the schools and districts we studied used extended-day programs to help all students learn to standards. For example, at Columbus Elementary School in Appleton (Wisconsin), the principal was able to secure a 21st Century Schools grant, which provided funds for an afterschool program. The grant was awarded to the school and the Boys and Girls Club jointly, the latter of which planned to provide the afterschool care. The principal knew that the most important part of having an afterschool program for her students who were struggling to learn to standards was to use this as time for learning math and reading, so she met with the Boys and Girls Club to talk about the goals and budget for the program. During this meeting, she made sure that two certified teachers, who would provide tutoring to struggling students, were included in the budget. The principal also obtained additional funding to help serve the homeless students at the school and hired two additional certified teachers to tutor those high-needs students. This strategy, combined with the tutoring described above, helped ensure that student needs were more adequately met, increasing their capacity to learn and have academic success.

Abbotsford (Wisconsin), a district profiled in Chapter 1, in which many of the struggling students are ELL, also obtained a 21st Century Schools grant. Using these funds, the school was able to provide extensive support for students outside of the regular school day. For one hour before school, two teachers came in and provided tutoring. After school, one teacher and two instructional aides were available for one and a half hours to provide tutoring.

Similarly, in Rosalia (Washington), teachers provided extended-day help for one half hour before school and one half hour after school. During both of these times, teachers were available to help students, primarily via one-to-one tutoring. The afterschool program was required for students with poor grades. In this way, the district ensured that students needing extra help the most received additional instruction in the core subjects from a certified teacher.

Extended learning time can also take the form of double periods of reading and math for students who are struggling to keep up. This strategy is most often used at the middle and high school level, where an elective course (or courses) is traded for the extra dose of reading and/or math. This is done on the theory that it is necessary to prioritize mastery of reading or math over subjects such as music or art, which while important in their own right, will not directly help students learn core, academic subjects such as reading and mathematics.

Park Middle School in Kennewick (Washington) was one of the many schools we visited during our work with schools that have doubled performance where extended learning time was one of the strategies. The principal at Park made it very clear, however, that *doubles*, as they called the extra period of reading and/or math that students who were struggling in these subjects were required to take, were not more of the same instruction in reading and/or math that students were receiving during their regular classroom time for these subjects. Instead, these double periods were staffed with teachers who were specialists in teaching the subject matter, teachers who knew other instructional strategies to help students learn concepts that they did not understand when they were introduced by the classroom teacher. To ensure that the students in need of a double period were identified quickly, the school (and other schools in the district) used frequent formative assessments. Students scoring below grade level were immediately shifted into doubles; it worked the other way, too, with students back at grade level immediately allowed to go back to their elective courses.

Another example of a school that used the doubles strategy and had success with low-income students is Elmont Junior/Senior High School. This school, previously referenced in this book as presenting at the Doubling Performance conference in July 2008 and also the subject of a book chapter (Chenoweth, 2007), made sure that students who were struggling with reading or math had more than one dose of it during the regular school day, thereby increasing these students' chances of success on standardized tests and in life.

While neither of the examples of schools offering double periods of math and/or reading listed above was explicitly funded through a reallocation of resources, an implicit reallocation of resources is at work here. By having teachers teach some students (those struggling to keep up) two periods of core subjects rather than one, the school effectively used more resources for core classroom teachers and fewer resources for electives.

SUMMER SCHOOL PROGRAM FOCUSED ON CORE INSTRUCTION

Particularly for students from low-income backgrounds, research has shown that having a long period of time in the summer without instruction in mathematics and reading can cause a backward slide in their knowledge and understanding of the concepts they need to master in order to learn to proficiency (Borman & Boulay, 2004; Borman et al., 2001; Cooper et al., 2000). Many of the schools and districts we studied were keenly aware of this fact, and thus, they allocated resources for the provision of summer school, especially for students at risk of not performing to proficiency.

Summer school was part of the strategy for struggling students in Rosalia. It was offered only for students below grade level or at risk of being below grade level, and it included an intensive focus on reading and mathematics using certified teachers in an attempt to ensure these students' success in the following school year. It is worth noting that this use of resources for struggling students represents a departure from past practices, when summer school was often viewed as an enrichment program for all kids. In many districts, when it became clear that some students needed additional instruction in core courses, enrichment activities were retained and instruction in the core was added. The fact that Rosalia made the decision to use their limited resources to fund summer school only for struggling students reflects district leaders' awareness and public support of the reality that in order to learn to standards, some students require more resources.

In Abbotsford, three weeks of summer school were offered using resources from the 21st Century Schools grant. While these summer classes were optional, the teachers often lured students into academic activities, disguising extra-help academic work with appealing titles and encouraging specific students to participate. The district found exactly what the research supports: This time spent on academics in the summer helps low-income students in particular to start the school year off in as good a position for learning as possible.

Madison (Wisconsin) is another district for which summer school was an important part of their extra-help strategies for ensuring the success of all students but particularly those at risk of falling behind. Students in the latter category were mandated to go to summer school and given instruction in courses that they must pass but had previously failed. In this way, the district maximized the chance that all students would succeed, and the district would meet its accountability standards.

In terms of resources in the above examples, summer school was sometimes funded by a grant—as in the case of Abbotsford and its 21st Century Schools grant—and sometimes funded by the district, which indicated its understanding of how critical this strategy was to the success of students in need of extra help. In the absence of district funding or grant money, it was difficult to find money to finance summer school since it occurs outside of the regular school year, and there is rarely money left over to be used for this purpose.

At one of the schools we visited in Arkansas for our work related to adequacy in that state, the principal lamented the fact that the district did not pay for summer school, and she was unable to obtain grant money to fund it. However, this principal knew how important a few weeks of core instruction in the summer could be for her low-income students, the ones research says fall behind without it. As a result, she described a process she had of saving teacher time whenever she could and *banking* it to be used to pay teachers to come in during the summer to teach summer school. Because she had to piece together the funding, she never knew from year to year how much time she would be able to offer it, but the past couple of years she had been able to fund it for two or three weeks.

SUMMARY AND CONCLUSION

There is no doubt that the extra-help strategies described in this chapter were a big part of the success of the schools we visited that doubled performance. In addition, tutoring during the regular school day was part of the comprehensive school designs that many of the schools we studied for the first edition of this book reallocated resources to fund. Because the research is clear on how effective these practices can be when focused on academic help, it would seem reasonable that these strategies might be built into the funding structure for any district or school committed to succeeding with students from a variety of backgrounds. As you will see in the next chapter, the evidence-based adequacy model is one method of staffing a school that includes all three of these explicit strategies for helping struggling students: tutoring, extended day, and summer school. Chapter 7 illustrates how resources can be allocated to the evidence-based model and explains all of its components.

Linking School Finance Adequacy to Doubling Performance[1]

From the district and school perspectives, it is good to know what works and to know that schools and districts can restructure themselves around a more powerful instructional-improvement process, such as the examples provided in previous chapters in this book, and allocate or reallocate the resources they have towards those new strategies. At some point in implementing new instructional-improvement strategies, districts and schools must address the reality of whether they have sufficient or adequate resources to deploy all elements of what they anticipate will be more effective strategies. Once these fiscal issues are confronted, systems begin raising the school finance adequacy question.

Indeed, over the last several years, states and the school-finance-policy-and-practice communities have moved from a focus on school finance equity, which dominated school finance for nearly the entire twentieth century, to that of adequacy, as courts and legislatures interpret the education clauses of state constitutions to require that the school finance system must provide each district, school, and student an *adequate* level of resources (see Odden & Picus, 2008, for an overview of these changes). *Adequate* has generally been defined as a level of funding that would allow each district and school to deploy a range of educational programs and strategies that would provide each student an equal opportunity to achieve to the state's education performance standards. It is becoming clear, however, that although there is evidence to suggest that large improvements in student performance can be produced, the country does not yet have the knowledge and professional expertise to teach all students to high and rigorous performance standards.

That is why some school finance scholars have been modifying the broader definition of school finance adequacy to something more tangible and attainable. In a 2008 study of school finance adequacy for the state of North Dakota, Lawrence O. Picus and Associates defined adequacy for that state as resources sufficient to enable districts and schools to "double student academic achievement" over a four- to six-year period (Odden, Picus, Goetz, & Aportela, 2008). With this definition, the Odden and Picus approach to school finance adequacy aligns well with the focus of this book, which has been on strategies and resource-allocation practices that result in a doubling of student performance. Indeed, as mentioned earlier, many of the school and district studies were conducted as part of several states' adequacy analyses. The school finance question, then, becomes one of the degrees to which the resources—recommended by the Picus and Associates' approach to school finance adequacy—align with the resources and strategies schools and districts have used to double performance. The remainder of this chapter addresses this issue.

Principals and superintendents can use the information in this chapter to consider the extent to which their district or school contains all of the ingredients of the evidence-based adequacy model. However, the first step in broaching the school finance aspect of doubling performance is to first do what the schools and districts in this book did—reallocate extant resources to the degree possible, utilizing the strategies and tactics that can produce a doubling of student performance. Chapter 7 of the Odden and Picus (2008) school finance text addresses this issue and references an online tool principals can use to allocate all staffing resources in their school to the evidence-based adequacy model. A link to this tool can also be found in the resource list at the end of this book.

APPROACHES TO SCHOOL FINANCE ADEQUACY

Although there are four major methods to determine school finance adequacy (for overviews, see Baker, Taylor, & Vedlitz, 2004; Guthrie & Rothstein, 1999; Odden, 2003), only the professional judgment and the evidence-based approaches specify in some detail a set of programs and strategies for prototypical elementary, middle, and high schools, as well as configurations of the central office, operations and maintenance, and transportation functions. The professional judgment approach primarily uses the professional knowledge of panels of educators to identify the recommended programs and strategies, while the evidence-based approach used by Picus and Associates uses evidence from research and best practices, and more recently, results from studies of schools and districts that have doubled performance, to frame its recommendations. Although the evidence-based approach starts with a set of core recommendations, the core recommendations often are changed during the school-finance-reform process in each state as policymakers, as well as education leaders and practitioners, review the recommendations and tailor them to the unique conditions, cultures, desires, and requirements of the particular state. The final set of strategies and their resource needs are the basis of the cost estimates derived for schools and districts in any particular state.

EVIDENCE-BASED APPROACH TO SCHOOL FINANCE ADEQUACY

The evidence-based approach to school finance adequacy has been used in Kentucky (Odden, Fermanich, et al., 2003), Arkansas (Odden, Picus, & Fermanich, 2003; Odden, Picus, & Goetz, 2006), Arizona (Odden, Picus, Fermanich, & Goetz, 2005), Wyoming (Odden, Picus, Goetz, et al., 2005), Washington (Odden, Picus, Goetz, Fermanich, & Mangan, 2006), Wisconsin (Odden, Picus, Archibald, et al. 2007), and most recently North Dakota (Odden, Picus, Goetz, & Aportela, 2008). The recommendations from the evidence-based approach have been used by the Arkansas and Wyoming legislatures to restructure their states' school finance structures and will be considered by North Dakota during the 2010 legislative session.

The basic approach of evidence-based studies is to identify individual, school-based programs and educational strategies that research has shown to improve student learning. Although the rigor of the evidence supporting the effectiveness for each recommendation varies, this approach only includes recommendations that are supported by solid, research evidence or best practices. Although the degree of effectiveness of any individual-recommended program can be debated, as can the sum total of all the recommendations, the evidence-based approach includes many strategies that both education researchers and practitioners argue should be part of any high performance school (see, for example, Stringfield, Ross, & Smith, 1996).

The evidence-based model includes the following (see the above referenced, evidence-based studies as well as Chapter 4 of Odden and Picus [2008] for the evidence supporting each of these recommendations):

1. Full-day kindergarten

2. Core-class sizes of 15 for Grades K–3 and class sizes of 25 for all other Grades 4–12 (Core is defined as the regular classroom teacher in elementary school and teachers of mathematics, science, reading/

English/writing, history, and world language in secondary schools. With these ratios, class sizes average 18 in the elementary school and 25 in middle and high schools.)

3. Specialist teachers to provide instruction in art, music, physical education, career technical education, and other noncore classes and in numbers adequate to cover a six-period day in middle schools with teachers teaching for just five periods, and four 90-minute block schedules in high schools with teachers teaching for just three blocks each day

4. At least one period (usually an hour) of planning and preparation time each day for all teachers in elementary, middle, and high schools

5. Pupil support staff including guidance counselors (one full-time equivalent [FTE] position for every 250 students in middle and high schools) and nurses, as well as additional pupil support to include social workers and family liaison personnel, the latter provided on the basis of one FTE position for every 100 at-risk students[2]

6. A full-time librarian and principal in every prototypical school, as well as two secretarial positions in the prototypical elementary (432 students) and middle school (450 students), and three secretaries in the prototypical high school (600 students), and sometimes an additional assistant principal in the prototypical high school

7. An ambitious set of professional-development resources including one instructional coach for every 200 students (3.0 FTE positions in a 600-student high school), at least 10 pupil-free days for professional development, which usually means extending the school year for teachers by several additional days, and $100 per pupil for trainers and other expenses related to professional development

8. Supervisory aides to cover recess, lunch, hall monitoring, and bus loading and unloading

9. About $200 per pupil for instructional materials, formative assessments, and supplies; $250 per pupil for technology and equipment; and $250 per pupil for student activities (sports, clubs, etc.)

10. $25 per pupil to provide extra strategies for gifted and talented students

11. A comprehensive range of extra-help strategies for students who need additional instructional assistance and extra time to achieve rigorous state proficiency standards including the following:

    a. Resources to provide one-to-one tutoring at the ratio of one FTE teacher-tutor position for every 100 at-risk students

    b. Extended-day resources to provide an eight- to nine-week summer program with up to six hours per day with academic help, at the ratio of one FTE position for every 30 at-risk students, assuming that only about 50 percent of at-risk students would participate, producing class sizes of 15

c. Summer school resources to provide up to six hours a day of an eight- to nine-week summer program with academic help for two-thirds of the time, at the ratio of one FTE position for every 30 at-risk students, assuming that only about 50 percent of at-risk students would need such extra help and would attend the program, to produce class sizes of 15

d. One additional FTE teacher position for every 100 English language learner (ELL) students (the bulk of whom also are at risk and trigger the first three, extra-help resources) primarily to provide instruction in English as a second language

e. One teacher FTE and 0.5 aide position for every 150 students to provide services for high-incidence but lower-cost students with disabilities (three certified positions for 450-student elementary and middle schools and four positions for a 600-student high school); the model also advocates full state funding of the entire costs of the high-cost, special-need students (assuming two percent of those with disabilities are in the high cost category

12. Substitute teacher resources at 10 days for each teacher and instructional facilitator position

13. Central office staff covering the superintendent's office, the business office, curriculum and pupil support, technology personnel, and an operations and maintenance director (a per-pupil figure derived from a prototypical 3,500 student district)

14. Additional resources for operations and maintenance, transportation, and food services

To show what all these core recommendations mean in terms of staff positions and dollars, the recommendations are often displayed as applied to prototypical elementary, middle, and high schools (see Schedule 1). However, in actual use, the core recommendations are *fit* to the student numbers and student demographics of each school in a state, so schools with more students than shown in the prototypical schools would have proportionately more resources, and schools with fewer students would receive fewer resources, though several core resources—principal, secretary, librarian—often are retained for smaller schools to address diseconomies of small school size. Furthermore, schools with larger concentrations and numbers of at-risk students would be eligible for a greater level of resources triggered by those higher pupil counts.

SCHEDULE 1

Recommendations for Adequate Resources for Prototypical Elementary, Middle, and High Schools

School Element	Elementary Schools	Middle Schools	High Schools
School Characteristics			
School configuration	K–5	6–8	9–12
Prototypical school size	432	450	600
Class size	K–3: 15; 4–5: 25	6–8: 25	9–12: 25
Full-day kindergarten	Yes	NA	NA
Number of teacher work days	195 teacher work days, including 10 days for professional development	190 teacher work days, including 10 days for professional development	190 teacher work days, including 10 days for professional development
Percentage poverty (free & reduced-priced lunch)	50%	50%	50%
Percentage ELL	10.6%	10.6%	10.6%
Personnel Resources			
1. Core teachers	24	18	24
2. Specialist teachers	20% more assuming a six-period day with each FTE teaching five periods: 4.8	20% more assuming a six-period day with each FTE teaching five periods: 3.6	33% more assuming a 90-minute block schedule with each FTE teaching three blocks a day: 8.0
3. Instructional facilitators/ coaches (ratio of one for every 200 students)	2.2	2.25	3.0
4. Tutors for struggling students	one for every 100 poverty students: 2.16	one for every 100 poverty students: 2.25	one for every 100 poverty students: 3.00
5. Teachers for ELL students	An additional teacher for every 100 ELL students 0.46	An additional teacher for every 100 ELL students 0.48	An additional teacher for every 100 ELL students 0.64
6. Extended day	1.8	1.875	2.5
7. Summer school	1.8	1.875	2.5
8. Students with mild disabilities	Three additional professional-teacher positions and 1.5 aide positions	Three additional professional-teacher positions and 1.5 aide positions	Four additional professional-teacher positions and 2.0 aide positions

School Element	Elementary Schools	Middle Schools	High Schools
9. Students with severe disabilities	100% state reimbursement minus federal funds	100% state reimbursement minus federal funds	100% state reimbursement minus federal funds
10. Resources for gifted/talented students	$25/student	$25/student	$25/student
11. Substitutes	10 days per FTE	10 days per FTE	10 days per FTE
12. Pupil support staff	1 for every 100 poverty students: 1.32 total	1 for every 100 poverty students plus 1.0 guidance/250 students: 3.18 total	1 for every 100 poverty students plus 1.0 guidance/250 students: 4.25 total
13. Supervisory aides	2.0	2.0	3.0
14. Librarian	1.0	1.0	1.0
15. Principal	1	1	1
16. School site secretary	1.0 secretary and 1.0 clerical	1.0 secretary and 1.0 clerical	1.0 secretary and 3.0 clerical
Dollar per Pupil Resources			
17. Professional development	*Included above:* Instructional facilitators 10 summer days *Additional:* $100/pupil for other PD expenses—trainers, conferences, travel, etc.	*Included above:* Instructional facilitators 10 summer days *Additional:* $100/pupil for other PD expenses—trainers, conferences, travel, etc.	*Included above:* Instructional facilitators 10 summer days *Additional:* $100/pupil for other PD expenses—trainers, conferences, travel, etc.
18. Technology and equipment	$250/pupil	$250/pupil	$250/pupil
19. Instructional materials, including textbooks, formative assessments	$200/pupil	$200/pupil	$200/pupil
20. Student activities	$250/pupil	$250/pupil	$250/pupil
Other Expenditures			
21. Operations and maintenance	A dollar/pupil figure	A dollar/pupil figure	A dollar/pupil figure
22. Transportation	A dollar/pupil figure	A dollar/pupil figure	A dollar/pupil figure
23. Food Services	A dollar/pupil figure	A dollar/pupil figure	A dollar/pupil figure

NOTE: ELL = English language learners; FTE = full-time equivalent; PD = professional development.

LINKAGE TO RESOURCES
NEEDED TO DOUBLE PERFORMANCE

It should be quite clear that the types of resources recommended by the evidence-based approach to school finance are very compatible with the programmatic strategies used by the schools and districts profiled in this book that have doubled performance. We should note that although both authors conducted some of the research on the schools and districts that doubled performance, we were somewhat but pleasantly surprised at the strong alignment between what the evidence-based approach to school finance adequacy had been recommending and the programs and strategies used by the districts and schools that have doubled performance.

Although indirect, the strong alignment was both support for the potential power of the overall set of recommendations themselves and a plausible answer to the question asked in every state where such an adequacy study had been conducted: "What kind of performance improvement can be expected if districts and schools had a level of resources that would enable them to deploy these strategies?" The answer that can now be given is, "a doubling of student performance on academic achievement tests." There is quantitative research that supports each individual recommendation, and there now is emerging qualitative research, much of it referenced and described in this book, showing that when combined, such resources and strategies can double student performance.

The fact is that the evidence-based recommendations were a series of individual program recommendations derived from evidence that each individual program or strategy—class sizes of 15 in Grades K–3, tutoring, summer school, professional development with coaching—had been shown by research to be effective, meaning linked to statistically significant improvements in student academic achievement. The evidence-based reports even provided effect sizes for each of the various programs, where the effect was how much more, in terms of a standard deviation of student performance, was produced in the various studies by the specific, individual program.

Many individuals in the various states asked whether the effect sizes of the individual programs could be added together to indicate the effect of implementing all the programs at once. Of course, that cannot be done, and there was no statistical answer to that question.

That is why, in part, we began a series of studies of schools and districts that had doubled performance. We wanted to learn from those practitioners on the ground exactly how it could be done. The goal was to identify the strategies deployed and their resource needs, so we could begin to link the recommendations from the school finance adequacy studies to achievable gains in student performance. As implied, we initially were somewhat stunned by the similarity of the programs and strategies and also pleasantly surprised by their strong alignment with the above adequacy recommendations.

In many of the places we studied, however, we found that districts and schools had doubled performance at one or two school levels (e.g., elementary and middle schools) and/or in just one or two subject areas (e.g., reading and mathematics) but not in all core subjects nor at all school levels. Furthermore, we found that such places had exhausted their level of resources and did not have resources to deploy these effective strategies for the other core subject areas (e.g., science and history) or for other grade levels (most often both middle and high schools). Sometimes, these strategies were funded by grants that, when the money ran out, schools and districts were unable to continue implementing the strategy. In such cases, their own programmatic, restructuring, and resource reallocation experiences provided them concrete arguments for both what new resources they needed (e.g., coaches for science or more professional development for high school teachers) and how much those additional resources would cost. Since the schools and districts had had such success deploying those resources for certain instructional-improvement strategies in some subjects and at some school levels, they were quite confident that similar types of strategies deployed in other subjects and at other school levels would have similarly large impacts on student achievement, and the cases that we and others have profiled testify to those assumptions. Practitioners might find the resource reallocation strategies presented in this book helpful in garnering as much money as possible to put toward instructional improvement.

CAUTIONS ABOUT LOCAL RESOURCE-USE PRACTICES

On the other hand, we would caution state policymakers that if a level of dollars sufficient to support all the strategies depicted in Schedule 1 were given to districts in a lump sum with no restrictions, then those resources would probably not be spent on those strategies and programs! Indeed, there have been several recent studies of that topic and the findings are sobering. In a study of resource-use practices at the school level from a random sample of 100 schools after the Arkansas adequacy oriented school finance, Mangan, Odden, and Picus (2007) found that local resource use supported more administration and more elective classes than in the Arkansas funding model, less professional development, less use of instructional coaches as part of ongoing professional development, and much less use of tutoring as a strategy for providing extra help to struggling students.

In a similar study, Odden, Picus, Aportela, Mangan, and Goetz (2008) found a similar pattern for Wyoming schools. Compared to the Wyoming funding model, schools employed fewer core teachers, more elective class teachers, large numbers of instructional aides, fewer certified teacher-tutors, less pupil support staff, and less professional development.

What both studies seemed to imply is that schools and districts on average have a different theory about how to improve student academic achievement than in the evidence-based funding model, which is highly aligned with the practices in the schools and districts that we and others have studied that have doubled performance. What schools and districts on average do is to put more resources into noncore elective classes; less into professional development and unless required, little into instructional coaches as part of professional development; and less into tutoring—the most effective, extra-help strategy for students struggling to learn to standards.

We should note that these more typical resource-use behaviors reflect practice over the past 50 years (see Odden and Picus, 2008).[3] They do not, however, represent the type of resource-use practices or instructional strategies that are successful in doubling student performance.

Thus, we would argue that state policymakers face a double challenge in the school finance adequacy context: identifying a level of resources that is adequate and designing an implementation strategy that would maximize the number of schools and districts using resources and deploying strategies in ways outlined in this book that should produce a doubling of student performance over a four- to six-year period. We do not offer a solution to this latter challenge; that is not the purpose of this book. But as states do move forward on the school finance adequacy terrain, they also need to design an implementation strategy that will maximize the chance that local districts and schools will use the funds—old and new—in the most effective ways to boost student learning.

GOOD ARGUMENTS FOR MORE MONEY

At this point, we only claim that there is a strong degree of consistency between the strategies and resources districts and schools have used to double performance and the strategies and resources provided by the evidence-based approach to school finance adequacy. This is good news.

This alignment, moreover, also provides districts and schools with ways to make concrete arguments for new money and for the level of funds that an adequate state school finance system should provide. Districts and schools should be able to claim that certain types of resources are needed to help them double student performance: decent class sizes; intensive professional development, including instructional coaches, tutors for one-to-one and small-group tutoring; academically oriented extended-day programs; and summer school. Districts and schools could show how far extant resources could be used to fund these strategies and be specific about how much more would be needed to deploy such strategies at all grade levels and in all core academic subjects. In this way, the information in this book can be used both to mount strategies at the district level to double student performance and simultaneously to mount advocacy strategies at the state level for more adequately funded school finance structures.

At the same time, states should work with district and school leaders, particularly those who actually have doubled student performance, to design structures and strategies to ensure that if adequate funding were provided, then district and school leaders would use those funds to implement strategies and programs that would dramatically improve student performance over time, rather than use the resources in the typical ways of the past that have not resulted in higher student achievement levels. Once those structures and strategies have been created, policymakers could then be optimistic that new resources would be used in effective and efficient ways.

SUMMARY AND FINAL COMMENTS

We began this book by noting that the education system in the United States is under pressure to dramatically improve student academic achievement. These performance increases are needed to provide all students, including students from lower-income and minority backgrounds, with the intellectual skills to be successful in work, family, and civic life in the 21st century—that is, to be ready after high school for work or more education needed in the growing, knowledge-based, global economy.

As the cases profiled in this book show, dramatic improvements in student achievement are possible. Often, they can be funded, at least in part, by reallocating resources away from less-effective strategies toward those that research has shown to be effective in schools. However, as this chapter has detailed, more resources might be needed, especially in states with low per-pupil spending, to reach the levels of performance expected by the No Child Left Behind Act that are much greater than the current situation. Once districts and schools have implemented the research-based strategies described in this chapter and throughout the book, they will likely be on an upward trajectory in terms of student achievement and will be able to make convincing arguments for the additional resources needed for additional learning gains.

It is important to be clear, however, that while having adequate resources and following the 10 steps for doubling performance listed in this book will both help increase the chances that student academic achievement will rise in a given district or school, these alone do not guarantee such success. This is true for two reasons.

First, as a precondition for launching any substantive strategy to double student performance, which focuses largely on the curriculum and instructional program, schools must initially establish an environment of order, discipline, and safety. In many of the cases profiled in Chapter 1, that was not an initial problem. But it was in the Granger High School case profiled by Chenoweth (2007). And it often is a challenge in many urban districts and schools. So if the school is in disarray, a precondition for engaging in more thoughtful curriculum and instructional change is to create an environment of discipline, order, and safety in the school.

Second, and related to the first point, to create and foster an environment of discipline, order, and safety or to carry out any of the 10 steps to doubling performance, schools and districts need talented, dedicated individuals in the key, strategic roles of teacher, principal, and district leader. In many districts in need of dramatic performance improvements, the individuals in the schools might not have been or be able to acquire the knowledge, skills, and expertise needed to implement the strategies designed to double student performance. In those cases, better talent is also a precondition. For example, there is considerable research on the need for more teacher and principal talent in many of the country's large urban districts. Furthermore, the Boyd, Lankford, Loeb, Rockoff, and Wyckoff (2007) study of New York City's five-year effort to increase the talent pool in its high-poverty schools showed it had produced a higher talent level as well as measurable gains in student achievement.

Furthermore, several cases on schools and districts that have doubled student performance are also examples of school reconstitution—that is, dramatic change in the teachers and principals working in the school. Dayton's Bluff (Chenoweth, 2007) and two of the K–8 schools in our reallocation book were schools that had been reconstituted. The Benwood Initiative in Chattanooga is another example of large-scale personnel change as part of a dramatic improvement effort (Chenoweth, 2007), and an unheralded aspect of the dramatic changes in New York City's Community District 2 under Anthony Alvarado's leadership was about a 50-percent change in teachers and a two-thirds change in the principals of the district's schools (Elmore & Burney, 1999).

In short, sufficient talent and human capital is important. Smart, capable, and well-trained professionals are needed to implement the 10 steps to double performance. If the talent pool is inadequate at the beginning, efforts to enhance the talent pool will need to be added to the overall strategy for it to be successful.

Once the talent is in place, a central focus of the districts and schools we studied was the creation of a continuous cycle of instructional improvement. To sustain the impressive gains detailed here, a continuous cycle of instructional improvement is necessary. This is true not only for the districts and schools we studied but also for most of the other studies of large-scale education improvement, which find that the key to producing continuous student achievement gains over several years toward the goal of having all students perform to proficiency is continuous instructional improvement. Whether described more generally as Step 3 of the change process described in Chapter 1 or as Steps 3, 4, and 5 in Chapter 3 of this book or the breakthrough toward expert and data-driven instructional change as articulated by Fullan, Hill, and Crevola (2006), the core of the education enterprise is instruction; and unless that changes in ways to allow all students to perform at high levels, the 10 steps will not produce the desired achievement improvements.

Moreover, the focus on instructional improvement drives resource use and educational costs. Indeed, a recent report on how to redesign American public school finance systems argues that the core for the architecture of the new school finance is creating a continuous cycle of instructional improvement in schools and districts and allocating resources to strengthen that central core function over time (Adams, 2008).

This book offers evidence that schools using many of the research-based strategies described in the evidence-based adequacy model have dramatically improved performance. Along with the knowledge that talent is key, it is our hope that the distillation of the experiences of these schools and districts into 10 steps to doubling performance and the strategies for allocating and reallocating resources according to these instructional priorities will help schools, districts, and even states build the sort of systems that can sustain the continuous instructional improvement needed to give all students in America the education they deserve.

NOTE

1. Portions of this chapter draw heavily from Odden, Picus, & Goetz (2007). This research was supported by the School Finance Redesign Project at the University of Washington's Center on Reinventing Public Education through funding by the Bill & Melinda Gates Foundation, Grant No. 29252. The views expressed herein are those of the authors and are not intended to represent the project, center, university, or foundation.

2. At-risk students are generally the number of students eligible for the federal free and reduced-price lunch program, often with adjustments for high school students where lunch eligibility is typically underreported.

3. We should also note that community pressures and parents often want small classes and extensive elective opportunities and often do not pressure for extra services to students struggling to learn, so that actual, resource-use practices—without state restrictions—reflect local political pressures.

Links to Web-Based Tools for School Leaders

1. The Wisconsin Idea Doubling Performance Conference
   This conference features in-depth presentations by leaders from around the country that have doubled student performance and closed the achievement gap on state tests over the past five to seven years. Visit this Web site for copies of PowerPoint presentations from the 2007 and 2008 conferences.
   http://www.education.wisc.edu/elpa/conferences/WILA/

2. The Education Trust
   The Education Trust works for the high academic achievement of all students, and the Educational Trust Web site has numerous resources related to the work discussed in this book.
   http://www2.edtrust.org/edtrust/

3. The Consortium for Policy Research in Education (CPRE) Web Site
   School Finance Redesign Report
   This Web resource can provide information on the degree to which your school could finance, through resource reallocation, the school-based adequacy model developed in Chapter 4 of the fourth edition of *School Finance: A Policy Perspective* (Odden & Picus, 2008).
   http://cpre.wceruw.org/finance/reports.php

4. Evidence-Based Adequacy as Applied to Wisconsin
   You can also visit the CPRE Web site to download a copy of the Wisconsin School Finance Adequacy Initiative Final Report.
   http://cpre.wceruw.org/

5. The Education Resource Strategies (ERS) District Resource Allocation Modeler (DREAM)
   The ERS DREAM helps school districts see how the strategic use of resources—people, time, and dollars—can impact the key levers of student performance.
   http://www.erstools.org/myDream/

References

Achilles, C. (1999). *Let's put kids first, finally: Getting class size right*. Thousand Oaks, CA: Corwin Press.

Adams, J. (2008). *Funding school success: How to align education resources with student learning goals*. Seattle: University of Washington, Evans School of Public Affairs, Center on Reinventing Public Education, School Finance Redesign Project.

Archibald, S., & Gallagher, H. A. (2002). A case study of professional development expenditures at a restructured high school. *Education Policy Analysis Archives, 10*(29), 1–24.

Baker, B., Taylor, L., & Vedlitz, A. (2004). *Measuring educational adequacy in public schools* (Report Prepared for the Texas Legislature Joint Committee on Public School Finance, the Texas School Finance Project). Retrieved August 28, 2008, from http://www.legis.state.tx.us

Blankstein, A. (2004). *Failure is not an option: Six principles that guide student achievement in high performing schools*. Thousand Oaks, CA: Corwin Press.

Borman, G. D., & Boulay, M. (Eds.). (2004). *Summer learning: Research, policies, and programs*. Mahwah, NJ: Lawrence Erlbaum.

Borman, G. D., & D'Agostino, J. V. (1996). Title I and student achievement: A meta-analysis of federal evaluation results. *Educational Evaluation and Policy Analysis, 18*(4), 309–326.

Borman, G. D., Rachuba, L., Hewes, G., Boulay, M., & Kaplan, J. (2001). Can a summer intervention program using trained volunteer teachers narrow the achievement gap? First-year results from a multiyear study. *ERS Spectrum, 19*(2), 19–30.

Boudett, K. P., City, E. A., & Murnane, R. (2007). *A step-by-step guide to using assessment results to improve teaching and learning*. Cambridge, MA: Harvard Education Press.

Boudett, K. P., & Steele, J. L. (2007). *Data wise in action: Stories of schools using data to improve teaching and learning*. Cambridge, MA: Harvard Education Press.

Boyd, D., Lankford, H., Loeb, S., Rockoff, J., & Wyckoff, J. (2007). *The narrowing gap in New York City teacher qualifications and its implications for student achievement in high-poverty schools*. Washington, DC: The Urban Institute, Center for Analysis of Longitudinal Data in Education Research.

Bransford, J., Brown, A., & Cocking, R. (1999). *How people learn*. Washington, DC: National Academy Press.

Chenoweth, K. (2007). *It's being done. Academic success in unexpected schools*. Cambridge, MA: Harvard Education Press.

Childress, S., Elmore, R., & Grossman, A. (2006). How to manage urban school districts. *Harvard Business Review, 84*(11), 55–68.

Childress, S., Elmore, R., Grossman, A., & Johnson, S. M. (2007). *Managing school districts for high performance.* Cambridge, MA: Harvard Education Press.

Cohen, D. K., & Hill, H. C. (2001). *Learning policy: When state education reform works.* New Haven, CT: Yale University Press.

Cohen, P., Kulik, J., & Kulik, C. (1982). Educational outcomes of tutoring: A meta-analysis of findings. *American Educational Research Journal, 19,* 237–248.

Cohen, D. K., Raudenbush, S. W., & Ball, D. L. (2002). Resources, instruction, and research. In R. Boruch & F. Mosteller (Eds.), *Evidence matters: Randomized trials in education research* (pp. 80–119). Washington, DC: The Brookings Institution.

Cooper, H., Charlton, K., Valentine, J. C., & Muhlenbruck, L. (2000). Making the most of summer school: A meta-analytic and narrative review. *Monographs of the Society for Research in Child Development, 65* (1, Serial No. 260).

Cooper, R., Slavin, R. E., & Madden, N. A. (1997). *Success for all: Exploring the technical, normative, political, and socio-cultural dimensions of scaling up.* Paper presented at the American Educational Research Association, Chicago.

Cunningham, P., & Allington, R. (1994). *Classrooms that work: They can all read and write.* New York: HarperCollins.

Donovan, S., & Bransford, J. (2005a). *How students learn—History in the classroom.* Washington, DC: National Research Council.

Donovan, S., & Bransford, J. (2005b). *How students learn—Mathematics in the classroom.* Washington, DC: National Research Council.

Donovan, S., & Bransford, J. (2005c). *How students learn—Science in the classroom.* Washington, DC: National Research Council.

Education Trust. (2006). *The power to change: High schools that help all students achieve.* Washington, DC: Author.

Educational Leadership. (2007, December/2008, January). [Entire Issue: Informative Assessment]. 65(4).

Elmore, R. F. (2002). *Bridging the gap between standards and achievement: The imperative for professional development in education.* Washington, DC: Albert Shanker Institute.

Elmore, R. F., & Burney, D. (1999). Investing in teacher learning: Staff development and instructional improvement. In L. Darling-Hammond & G. Sykes (Eds.), *Teaching as the learning profession: Handbook of policy and practice* (pp. 263–291). San Francisco: Jossey-Bass.

Farkas, G. (1998). Reading one-to-one: An intensive program serving a great many students while still achieving. In J. Crane (Ed.), *Social programs that work* (pp. 75–109). New York: Russell Sage Foundation.

Farkas, G. (1999). *Can Title I attain its goal?* Brookings Papers on Education Policy. Washington, DC: The Brookings Institution.

Fermanich, M. (2003). *School resources and student achievement: The effect of school-level resources on instructional practices and student outcomes in Minneapolis public schools.* Unpublished doctoral dissertation, University of Wisconsin–Madison.

Fermanich, M., Mangan, M. T., Odden, A. R., Picus, L. O., Gross, B., & Rudo, Z. (2006). *Washington learns: Successful districts study.* Analysis prepared for the

K–12 Advisory Committee of Washington Learns. Available at http://www.washingtonlearns.wa.gov/materials/SuccessfulDistReport9–11–06 Final_000.pdf

Fielding, L., Kerr, N., & Rosier, P. (2004). *Delivering on the promise . . . of the 95% reading and math goals.* Kennewick, WA: The New Foundation Press.

Fullan, M. (2001). *The new meaning of educational change.* New York: Teachers College Press.

Fullan, M., Hill, P., & Crevola, C. (2006). *Breakthrough.* Thousand Oaks, CA: Corwin Press.

Gallagher, H. A. (2002). Elm Street School: A case study of professional development expenditures. *Education Policy Analysis Archives, 10*(28), 1–32.

Garet, M. S., Birman, B., Porter, A., Desimone, L., & Herman, R. (1999). *Designing effective professional development: Lessons from the Eisenhower program.* Washington, DC: United States Department of Education.

Goldhaber, D., & Anthony, E. (2005). Can teacher quality be effectively assessed? National Board Certification as a signal of effective teaching. Washington, DC: Department of Education.

Goldhaber, D., Perry, D., & Anthony, E. (2004). The National Board for Professional Teaching Standards (NBPTS) process: Who applies and what factors are associated with NBPTS certification? *Educational Evaluation and Policy Analysis, 26*(4), 259, 22–280.

Grissmer, D. (1999). Class size: Issues and new findings [Entire issue]. *Educational Evaluation and Policy Analysis, 21*(2).

Grubb, N. (2007). Dynamic inequality and intervention: Lessons from a small country. *Phi Delta Kappan, 89*(2), 105–114.

Guthrie, J. W., & Rothstein, R. (1999). Enabling "adequacy" to achieve reality: Translating adequacy into state school finance distribution arrangements. In H. Ladd, R. Chalk, & J. Hansen (Eds.), *Equity and adequacy in education finance: Issues and perspectives* (pp. 209–259). Washington, DC: National Academy Press.

Gutierrez, R., & Slavin, R. (1992). Achievement effects of the nongraded elementary school: A best evidence synthesis. *Review of Educational Research, 62,* 333–376.

Haynes, N., Emmons, C., & Woodruff, D. (1998). School development program effects: Linking implementation to outcomes. *Journal of Education for Students Placed At Risk, 3*(1), 71–85.

Hightower, A., Knapp, M., Marsh, J., & McLaughlin, M. (2002). *School districts and instructional renewal.* New York: Teachers College Press. (See articles especially Chapters 2, 3, and 10)

Huberman, M., & Miles, M. (1984). *Innovation up close.* New York: Plenum Press.

Jordan, N. C. (2007). The need for number sense. *Educational Leadership, 65*(2), 63–66.

Joyce, B., & Calhoun, E. (1996). *Learning experiences in school renewal: An exploration of five successful programs.* Eugene, OR: ERIC Clearinghouse on Educational Management.

Joyce, B., & Showers, B. (2002). *Student achievement through staff development* (3rd ed.). Alexandria, VA: Association for Supervision and Curriculum Development.

Kreuger, A. (2002). Understanding the magnitude and effect of class size on student achievement. In L. Mishel & R. Rothstein (Eds.), *The class size debate* (pp. 7–35). Washington, DC: Economic Policy Institute.

Loeb, S., Bryk, A., & Hanushek, E. (2007). *Getting down to facts: School finance and governance in California.* Stanford, CA: Stanford University.

Loucks-Horsley, S., Love, N., Stiles, K., Mundry, S., & Hewson, P. (2003). *Designing professional development for teachers of science and mathematics* (2nd ed.). Thousand Oaks, CA: Corwin Press.

Mangan, M. T. (2007). *School level use in Arkansas: A statewide study.* Unpublished doctoral dissertation, University of Wisconsin-Madison.

Mangan, M. T., Odden, A. R., & Picus, L. O. (2007). School level resource use in Arkansas following an adequacy oriented school finance reform. *Education Finance and Policy.* Manuscript submitted for review.

Mangan, M., & Stoelinga, S. R. (2008). *Effective teacher leadership.* New York: Teachers College Press.

Mason, D. A., & Burns, R. (1996). Simply no worse and simply no better may simply be wrong: A critique of Veenman's conclusion about multigrade classes. *Review of Educational Research, 66*(3), 307–322.

Mason, D. A., & Stimson, J. (1996). Combination and nongraded classes: Definitions and frequency in twelve states. *Elementary School Journal, 96*(4), 439–452.

Mathes, P. G., & Fuchs, L. S. (1994). The efficacy of peer tutoring in reading for students with mild disabilities: A best-evidence synthesis. *School Psychology Review, 23,* 59–80.

McRobbie, J., Finn, J. D., & Harman, P. (1998). *Class size reduction: Lessons learned from experience* (Policy Brief No. 23). San Francisco: WestEd.

Miles, K. H., & Darling-Hammond, L. (1998). Rethinking the allocation of teaching resources: Some lessons from high-performing schools. *Educational Evaluation and Policy Analysis, 20*(1), 9–29.

Miles, K. H., & Frank, S. (2007). *The strategic school: How to make the most of your school's people, time, and money.* Thousand Oaks, CA: Corwin Press.

Miles, K. H., Odden, A. R., Archibald, S., & Fermanich, M. (2004). Inside the black box of school district spending on professional development: Lessons from five urban districts. *Journal of Education Finance. 30*(1), 1–26.

Miller, S. D. (2003). Partners in reading: Using classroom assistants to provide tutorial assistance to struggling first-grade readers. *Journal of Education for Students Placed At Risk, 8*(3), 333–349.

Mohrman, S. (1994). Large scale change. In S. Mohrman & P. Wohlstetter (Eds.), *School-based management: Organizing for high performance.* San Francisco: Jossey-Bass.

Mohrman, S. A., & Cummings, T. G. (1989). *Self-designing organizations: Learning how to create high performance.* Reading, MA: Addison-Wesley.

Murnane, R., & Levy, F. (1996). *Teaching the new basic skills.* New York: Free Press.

Musti-Rao, S., & Cartledge, G. (2007). Delivering what urban readers need. *Educational Leadership, 6*(2), 56–61.

Newmann, F., & Associates. (1996). *Authentic achievement: Restructuring schools for intellectual quality.* San Francisco: Jossey-Bass.

Odden, A. R. (Ed.). (1991). *Education policy implementation.* Albany: State University of New York Press.

Odden, A. R. (2003). Equity and adequacy in school finance today. *Phi Delta Kappan, 85*(2), 120–125.

Odden, A., & Archibald. S. (2000). Reallocating resources to support higher student achievement: An empirical look at five sites. *Journal of Education Finance. 25*(4), 545–564.

Odden, A. R., & Archibald, S. (2001a). Committing to class-size reduction and finding the resources to implement it: A case study of resource reallocation in Kenosha, Wisconsin. *Education Policy Analysis Archives. 9*(30). Available at http://epaa.asu.edu/epaa/v9n30.html

Odden, A. R., & Archibald, S. (2001b). *Reallocating resources: How to boost student achievement without spending more.* Thousand Oaks, CA: Corwin Press.

Odden, A. R., Archibald, S., Fermanich, M., & Gallagher, H. A. (2002). A cost framework for professional development. *Journal of Education Finance, 28*(1), 51–74.

Odden, A. R., Archibald, S., Fermanich, M., & Gross, B. (2003). Defining school-level expenditure structures that reflect educational strategies. *Journal of Education Finance 28*(3): 323–356.

Odden, A., Fermanich, M., & Picus, L. O. (2003). *A state-of-the-art approach to school finance adequacy in Kentucky* (Report Prepared for the Kentucky State Department of Education). North Hollywood, CA: Lawrence O. Picus and Associates.

Odden, A. R., & Picus, L. O. (2004). *School finance: A policy perspective* (3rd ed.). New York: McGraw-Hill.

Odden, A. R., & Picus, L. O. (2008). *School finance: A policy perspective* (4th ed.). New York: McGraw Hill.

Odden, A. R., Picus, L. O., Aportela, A., Mangan, M. T., & Goetz, M. (2008). *School level resource use in Wyoming following an adequacy oriented school finance reform: Findings from a fifty percent random sample.* Report submitted to the Wyoming Legislature.

Odden, A. R., Picus, L. O., Archibald, S., Goetz, M., Aportela, A., & Mangan, M. T. (2007). *Moving from good to great in Wisconsin: Funding schools adequately and doubling student performance.* Madison: University of Wisconsin, Wisconsin Center for Education Research, Consortium for Policy Research in Education.

Odden, A. R., Picus, L. O., & Fermanich, M. (2003). *An evidence-based approach to school finance adequacy in Arkansas* (Prepared for the Interim Legislative Committee of School Finance). Lawrence O. Picus & Associates, Inc. Retrieved June 7, 2004, from http://www.arkleg.state.ar.us/data/education/FinalArkansasReport.pdf

Odden, A. R., Picus, L. O., Fermanich, M., & Goetz, M. (2005). *An evidence-based approach to school finance adequacy in Arizona* (Prepared for the Steering Committee of the Arizona School Finance Adequacy Study). Phoenix: Rodel Charitable Foundation of Arizona.

Odden, A. R., Picus, L. O., & Goetz, M. (2006). *Recalibrating the Arkansas school funding structure* (Prepared for the Adequacy Study Oversight Sub-Committee of the House and Senate Interim Committees on Education of the Arkansas General Assembly). Little Rock.

Odden, A. R., Picus, L. O., & Goetz, M. (2007). *Paying for school finance adequacy with the national average expenditure per pupil* (Working paper 2). Seattle: University of Washington, Evans School of Public Policy, Center on Reinventing Public Education, School Finance Redesign Project. To be included in a collected volume, Funding student success, J. Adams, (Ed.), forthcoming.

Odden, A. R., Picus, L. O., Goetz, M., & Aportela, A. (2008). *Funding schools adequately in North Dakota: Resources to double student performance* (Prepared for the North Dakota Education Improvement Commission). North Hollywood, CA: Lawrence O. Picus & Associates.

Odden, A. R., Picus, L. O., Goetz, M., Fermanich, M., & Mangan, M. T. (2006). *An evidence-based approach to school finance adequacy in Washington.* (Report prepared for Washington Learns). Available at http://www.washington learns.wa.gov/materials/EvidenceBasedReportFina19–11–06.pdf

Odden, A. R., Picus, L. O., Goetz, M., Fermanich, M., Seder, R. C., Glenn, W., & Nelli, R. (2005). *An evidence-based approach to recalibrating Wyoming's block grant school funding formula.* Report prepared for the Wyoming Select Committee on Recalibration, Cheyenne, WY.

Office of Educational Research and Improvement. (1996). *The uses of time for teaching and learning (Studies of education reform).* Washington, DC: U.S. Department of Education.

Pavan, B. (1992). Recent research on nongraded schools: The benefits of non-graded schools. *Educational Leadership, 50*(2), 22–25.

Reynolds, A. J., & Wolfe, B. (1999). Special education and school achievement: An exploratory analysis with a central-city sample. *Educational Evaluation and Policy Analysis, 21*(3), 249–269.

Shanahan, T. (1998). On the effectiveness and limitations of tutoring in reading. *Review of Research in Education, 23,* 217–234.

Shanahan, T, & Barr, R. (1995). Reading recovery: An independent evaluation of the effects of an early instructional intervention for at-risk learners. *Reading Research Quarterly, 30*(4), 958–997.

Sherry, A. (2007, September 23). Rural school districts learn to flourish. *Denver Post,* p. A1.

Shulman, J. H., & Sato, M. (Eds). (2006). *Mentoring teachers toward excellence: Supporting and developing highly qualified teachers.* San Francisco: Jossey-Bass in partnership with WestEd.

Silva, E. (2007). *On the clock: Rethinking the way schools use time.* Washington, DC: Education Sector.

Slavin, R., Karweit, N., & Madden, N. (1989). *Effective programs for students at risk.* Boston: Allyn & Bacon.

Slavin, R., Madden, N., Dolan, L., & Wasik, B. (1996). *Every child, every school.* Thousand Oaks, CA: Corwin Press.

Spillane, J. P., Halverson, R., & Diamond, J. B. (2001). Investigating school leadership practice: A distributed perspective. *Educational Researcher, 30*(3), 23–27.

Stringfield, S., & Datnow, A. (1998). Scaling up school restructuring and improvement designs [Entire issue]. *Education and Urban Society, 30*(3).

Stringfield, S., Ross, S., & Smith, L. (1996). *Bold plans for school restructuring: The new American schools designs.* Mahwah, NJ: Lawrence Erlbaum.

Supovitz, J. (2006). *The case for district based reform.* Cambridge, MA: Harvard Education Press.

Supovitz, J., & Turner, H. M. (2000). The effects of professional development on science teaching practices and classroom culture. *Journal of Research in Science Teaching, 37*(9), 963–980.

Thayer, J. (2004). *Professional development: Costs and effectiveness in one rural district.* Unpublished doctoral dissertation, University of Wisconsin–Madison.

Torgeson, J. K. (2004). Avoiding the devastating downward spiral. *American Educator, 28*(3), 6–19, 45–47.

Veenman, S. (1995). Cognitive and noncognitive effects of multigrade and multi-age classes: A best evidence synthesis. *Review of Educational Research, 65,* 319–381.

Vinovskis, M. (1999). Do federal compensatory education programs really work? A brief historical analysis of Title I and Head Start. *American Journal of Education, 107*(3), 187–209.

Wasik, B., & Slavin, R. E. (1993). Preventing early reading failure with one-to-one tutoring: A review of five programs. *Reading Research Quarterly, 28,* 178–200.

Index

CORWIN PRESS

The Corwin Press logo—a raven striding across an open book—represents the union of courage and learning. Corwin Press is committed to improving education for all learners by publishing books and other professional development resources for those serving the field of PreK–12 education. By providing practical, hands-on materials, Corwin Press continues to carry out the promise of its motto: **"Helping Educators Do Their Work Better."**